# From the Shores of Ship Creek
## Stories of Anchorage's First 100 Years

By Charles Wohlforth

**Todd Communications** – Anchorage

*To Barbara*

Soft Cover ISBN: 978-1-57833-603-6
Hard Cover ISBN: 978-1-57833-607-4

First printing February, 2015
Second printing May, 2015

Printed by Everbest Printing Co., Ltd., in Guangzhou, China through Alaska Print Brokers, Anchorage, Alaska.

Design: Vered R. Mares, Todd Communications
Editors: David Holthouse and Flip Todd
Photographs: Used by permission
Front and Back cover photos are by Jim Lavrakas, from his book *Snap Decisions: 30 years as an Alaskan News Photographer*, and are used with other photos as noted in the book, though the generosity of the Alaska Dispatch News.

Published by
Todd Communications
611 E. 12th Ave., Suite 102
Anchorage, Alaska 99501
**Phone: (907) 274-TODD (8633)** • Fax: (907) 929-5550
email: sales@toddcom.com • WWW.ALASKABOOKSANDCALENDARS.COM

with other offices in Juneau and Fairbanks, Alaska

ALASKA
HUMANITIES
FORUM

# Contents

# Introduction

Looking for the heart of Anchorage, it's tempting to return to the beginnings, a tent camp on the banks of Ship Creek where gold rush-tested entrepreneurs opened up shop in expectation that a new government railroad would produce a city. Or even farther back, to the visit of the English explorer Captain James Cook, who fancied in his journal that this impossibly remote land at the rim of the known world would someday be a population center. Or to the first people, the Dena'ina, who used the area as hunters, fishermen and traders, and defended it fiercely in war.

Anchorage stands where it does because of the unique geography those early occupants recognized. It is a natural center of commerce and national defense and a hub for transportation by land, water and air. But despite the obvious worth of this flat land in the lap of the Chugach Mountains, the city's heart cannot be found so easily. In its first century, the essence of the city has been more complex and interesting than that, embodied in the flow of people streaming through its depot, roads and airport. Anchorage is about change, dynamism and the ability to absorb and enrich new people. Anchorage is much more than a piece of real estate. It's an attitude.

The generations populating Anchorage over a century shared a common orientation to the future. At a century old, the city is still changing rapidly, with a new migration of ethnically diverse residents from many cultural traditions. The nation's most completely integrated high school is in Anchorage, as well as its most diverse residential neighborhood. For long-time residents who remember a plain white city, the new population comes as a surprise and, for many, a source of pride. The promise of Anchorage continues. New pioneers arriving from Samoa, the Philippines and dozens of other distant places come with the same aspirations as those who came to build the railroad, fight World War II, defend against the Soviet Union, and cross Alaska with an oil pipeline.

The pride comes in part from hearing, for example, why a Hmong refugee from Laos chose Anchorage for home. The beauty of the mountains, the safe, clean streets with light traffic, the good public schools, extraordinary recreation opportunities, and the promise that hard workers can find jobs and start businesses. Our mayors of recent decades talk about the same qualities in much the same terms. The Anchorage Economic Development Corporation recently adopted the goal of making Anchorage the number one city to live, work and play in the nation. No one laughed. Most residents are here by choice and already know Anchorage compares favorably to other cities.

Having arrived in Anchorage as a toddler in 1966, I've lived roughly half the city's 100 years of history in my 50-some years of life. Anchorage-grown adults remain in the minority, but we are gaining in numbers. We've seen how the city has developed through convulsive booms and disastrous busts, and has fought its way through issues about governance, taxation, community planning, race and sexual orientation. We are aware of the city's shortcomings as well as its opportunities. At times, I think I know too much. And then I encounter tourists walking the coastal trail, agog in the sun and scenery, grinning at the wildlife and the families on bikes and the athletes running by, and I see my hometown once again with fresh eyes. We are so lucky.

As a writer of more than ten books and countless articles, I've had many opportunities to capture Anchorage in words. In travel books, I've extolled the Alaska that is within reach in our mountains and at hand in our large parks. In history and biography, I've traced, with our most important leaders, the struggles and miracles of the city's growth. As an essayist and reporter, I've retold hundreds of amazing, tragic and inspiring stories. Now I'm faced with the task of freezing the city's gush of change on these unmoving pages, a task something like telling the story of a river by dipping from its stream.

But the task is not impossible, because I have the tool of storytelling. Anchorage is about change, about people going somewhere. Stories are about that, too. They're how we organize our personal experience of the world, gathering up the swirl of our experiences into material we can understand and communicate to others. Many kinds of expression can reflect history, but stories are the best way to make sense of it. Every story has a beginning, middle and end; it has characters with motivations; and it has conflict and antagonists. Every story depends on details, a place, a time and how it smelled, sounded and felt. A good story can recreate history in the listener's imagination more completely than the most carefully restored house.

*From the Shores of Ship Creek, Stories of Anchorage's First 100 Years* uses the stories of fifteen people who lived here as lenses to view the broader sweep of the city's growth; thirteen have their own chapters, while two share the final chapter. This is not a comprehensive history of Anchorage. It is neither an academic's portrait of the city nor a booster's polishing of images. *From the Shores of Ship Creek* is a collection of essays about individuals whose lives reflect the phases of the city's life.

These characters are people of their times. In some cases, I could have chosen more important or accomplished individuals. In my research I encountered many anecdotes about Anchorage I wanted to repeat, some of them funnier or more poignant than the stories I did include. Many other important topics would have belonged in a comprehensive history. The hardest part of writing this book was excluding material that wanted to crowd its way in. But I fought hard to keep the stories clean and fast-moving.

The motivation for this fight was to keep the focus on Anchorage. After 100 years, we can discern the stages of the city's development like the growth of a child into an adult. The stories each help envision the stages in that process.

Several themes flow through the city's story to make it the place it is today.

Today, Anchorage is undeniably permanent. At first, and for many years, that was not the case. Steve McCutcheon, who could remember the days of 1915 when C Street was a dirt path, said Anchorage didn't become permanent until oil was found on the Kenai Peninsula in the late 1950s. Others would say the military build-up of the 1940s and 1950s cemented Anchorage in the world. Whatever date is chosen, it's remarkable that for at least its first thirty years the city remained in childhood, its success or failure in doubt.

Anchorage's journey toward permanence was a struggle because of the odd way the city was incubated and nurtured by the federal government. As the book explains, the very location and existence of Anchorage came about because of political decisions in Washington, D.C., about building the Alaska Railroad, with only tenuous connections to economic reality. It soon became obvious that the railroad would have far less business than needed to justify its cost. It survived on large annual appropriations for operations until the drive to build World War II defenses suddenly made the railroad and the town essential.

The federal government ran the town for the first five years. That's why the city didn't incorporate until 1920. Until well after statehood in 1959, federal spending provided the overwhelming majority of economic activity. When the Good Friday Earthquake hit in 1964, halfway through the city's first century, military intervention and federal investment brought Anchorage back to life. Only in the last half of the city's life has it attained an economic base aside from the federal government, although the military remains a mainstay.

The city came to life through the intention of the people who moved here. Early city leaders wanted the city to be the center of Alaska and campaigned vigorously for military bases, an Alaska Native hospital, aviation facilities and government and corporate headquarters. They were Americans and wanted Anchorage to be the threshold for the rest of the United States into Alaska. An old insult—that Anchorage isn't part of Alaska, but you can see it from there—would not have bothered the downtown Anchorage businessmen who promoted the city. They wanted Anchorage to be an urban outpost in the wilderness, as much like neighborhoods in the Lower 48 as possible.

But a big part of our story is the tension between that vision and the desire of others in Anchorage for it to be more like Alaska than America. The most profound and longest-lasting conflicts in the city's history arise from that difference. Beginning in the 1950s, residents inside the old city, concentrated in the downtown area, hoped to expand their tidy, well-planned American city across the Anchorage bowl. Residents outside the city fought that spread, partly to avoid taxation, but also because their values of Alaskan pioneering independence didn't match the city's tidy grid of planning and public services. A truce came with unification of the city and borough in 1975 and creation of a unique local government that allows different areas of the municipality to live with different levels of service and different lifestyles.

But the question of whether Anchorage was more like America or Alaska continued as communication, trade and travel connecting the city to the rest of the United States became easier and national corporations brought their brands. The explosion of ethnic diversity over the last quarter century largely settled the question. Once again, the nation's most mobile and ambitious people came to Anchorage. These were the city's new pioneers. Today, the gold pan pioneer image reflects the reality of Anchorage as accurately as a cowboy in downtown Dallas, a Spanish missionary in San Francisco, or a cod fisherman on the streets of Boston.

Today, a strong consensus exists among Anchorage leaders about what sort of city we are, where we are going, and the qualities that will bring us to a successful future. It's a good time for the centennial.

But I doubt there is a consensus about where the heart of Anchorage lies. At the crossing of a Nordic ski trail and dog mushing trail in Far North Bicentennial Park? In the fragrant dining room of a Vietnamese Pho restaurant? Overlooking the glistening Inlet from the penthouse of an oil company high-rise? In the autumn scent of salmon smoking as it wafts through a suburban neighborhood of wide streets and green lawns? It's all essentially Anchorage, but for everyone the perspective and the experience itself seems quite different. We don't have an Eiffel Tower, a Golden Gate Bridge or a Broadway theater district.

But Anchorage does have a heart, a strong one. It's the heart of the future: of optimism and openness, the energy of youth and the belief in the new. There is a familiar image for that heart of Anchorage that everyone can recognize: the pink light that comes over the Chugach Mountains before dawn on a winter morning. Everyone has seen the ridges picked out by an unseen rising sun from the windshield of a car on the way to work or school. At that moment, we are all one, all going our different directions, with different concerns, hopes and beliefs, but all challenging the morning in this spectacular landscape where anything seems possible.

Here are the stories of people who lived under that mountain dawn for a century, and how they made a city here.

*—Charles Wohlforth, summer 2014*

# Chapter 1

## Shem Pete: A Place Called Dgheyay Kaq'

In the winter of 1914, Shem Pete, a teenage Dena'ina boy from the village of Tsat'ukegh, on the Susitna River, received a rifle as a gift from his mother. They went up the frozen Susitna by sled to the mining town of Talkeetna, where Shem shot fourteen black bear over the course of the next spring. In June they paddled a dory across Cook Inlet to Dgheyay Kaq' with the dried bear hides to sell to people who had suddenly arrived there, and who now were calling the place "Ship Creek" in their language.

Shem Pete in Anchorage, early 1920s. Photo provided by Jim Fall, courtesy of Alexandra Allowan

The flat land at the mouth of the creek had been, up to that point, thickly wooded with spruce, with just a few cabins. Jack and Nellie Brown lived nearest the creek. Jack was a ranger for Chugach National Forest, which encompassed the entire area south of Knik Arm. Just north at Tak'at was a fish camp belonging to the Stephan family of Knik and to the south more camps at every workable spot. The whole bowl from the mudflats up to the peaks of the mountains provided food for the upper Cook Inlet Dena'ina.

In 1915, several thousand new people arrived on boats that anchored off the creek. It was a good place to anchor among the swift currents and shoals of Knik Arm. At first that was the only noteworthy fact about the spot, which otherwise looked like so many others along a shore where creeks meander through the mud flats. It made sense to call the instant town that sprouted there "Knik Anchorage."

Decades later, Shem remembered his visit to the brand new town.

"They had the store in the tent. They carry the coat, dress, pants and shirt. They put it over our neck. They hold our back. 'That's big enough for you. Just right. Just right. Fifty cents. Sixty cents. Nice one seventy-five cents.' We buy, and I got a job in the restaurant. I was fourteen years old.

*Family of Knik Chief Nicholai, 1918. Photograph by H.G. Kaiser. Archives and Special Collections, Consortium Library, University of Alaska Anchorage.*

"And they burn and cut the trees. It's full of smoke, fire, nighttime. They like to work the nighttime, too. It's too hot daytime, June month, so a lot of people working. And I work in the restaurant. For about two weeks. And they play cards. Lots of gambling in the tent.

"And so we go back to Susitna in the dory. We tell the story, 'We see lots of white people. There's smoke all over in [Anchorage] there now.' At that time it was all full of trees and willows. Everything they cut down. Nights and days they work."

A picture of Shem Pete in Anchorage a few years later shows him, sharp-dressed, a cigarette hanging from his lower lip and an attitude on his face. He was a brilliant and self-assured man who remained proudly Dena'ina while everything around him changed. Shem was born in Tsat'ukegh when the Dena'ina way of life prevailed. Renamed Susitna Station, the village grew into an important river and Iditarod Trail supply town, then withered away after many residents died in the flu epidemic of 1918 and commerce petered out on the trail and river. Shem helped bury the last Dena'ina resident of Susitna Station in 1965. By then, only western clothes were worn on this land. Only urban life was lived in the place now known as Anchorage.

By the time Shem died in 1989, in his 90s, he alone remembered 350 place names from the region, place names with meanings that said what was done or remembered there. Dghelishla, a navigational landmark and sacred mountain of mourning, became Mount Susitna. The newcomers even made up a legend for the mountain, which they called Sleeping Lady, and printed that as if it came from tradition. The land is still here, but, like a computer disk overwritten with new files, it absorbed a new culture from new people mostly oblivious that anyone ever lived here before.

The Upper Cook Inlet Dena'ina did. They thrived here for centuries, holding the land against all enemies. They numbered in the thousands and lived richly as fishermen, hunters and traders. Perhaps a thousand years ago they had come through mountain passes from the Interior, bringing the Athabascans' land-based way of life to the coast, which they adapted only partially to the marine environment. They always remained partly mountain people, but also learned the tools of the seafaring Aluutiq from farther south, such as use of seal skin boats. The Dena'ina people of Knik Arm and the Matanuska River were the K'enaht'ana band. In the area that became Anchorage the only K'enaht'ana winter village was Idlughet, now known as Eklutna.

Shem Pete became a messenger from the past, carrying the knowledge of that old world into this new one. In the fall of 1978, Jim Fall set to work receiving the message. He was studying anthropology. On the advice of linguist Jim Kari, he went to a cabin on Nancy Lake where Shem and his son Billy were living and began asking them questions and recording what they said. He stayed a year.

"They liked to tell stories," Jim recalls. "They got tired of me after a while, a little bit, but they needed somebody to help them out. I would do things for them. In the Dena'ina tradition, elders, especially knowledgeable older elders, would be visited by younger men. There's even a term for it. It's called ukilaqa. It means, 'his helper,' and that's what I was. I was a young helper to Shem Pete and Billy Pete. So I would do chores for them, and in return they told me stories and would answer my questions. In a lot of ways it was quite a traditional relationship."

Traditional Dena'ina people lived during the winter in villages of large houses called nichiłs, with roofs of birch bark and walls of spruce logs, which were split so the inside surface was smooth. Several families slept on platforms around the edges and a fire burned in the center. In the spring they left for fish camps all along the shore. Fish camps lay at spots now known as Cairn Point (Tak'at), just north of the Port of Anchorage, at Fish Creek, at Point Woronzof and Point Campbell. If the winter had been long and food scarce, they went first to the mouth of Ship Creek to gather boney needlefish, the first protein of spring.

In May and June fishermen dipped king salmon from the murky Cook Inlet waters

The village of Tyonek, on the west side of Cook Inlet, 1898. The elevated building is a food-storage cache. Photo by the U.S. Army exploratory expedition led by Edwin F. Glenn. University of Alaska Anchorage Archives.

while standing on scaffolds of logs on the beach that allowed them to stay just above the water through the wide tidal cycle. Families worked together to clean and dry the fish for storage. Spring also was the time to trade with the Susitna River Dena'ina for eulachon (also known as hooligan) at a place known as Dilhi Tunch'del'usht Beydegh, which translates as "Point Where We Transport Eulachon," and now is called Point MacKenzie.

In the summer the K'enaht'ana Dena'ina harvested salmon from traps and weirs in the many creeks and rivers that run across the Anchorage bowl and on Knik Arm. Stakes driven into the creek bed supported structures to corral the fish, weighted by heavy rocks tied to braided roots. After putting up salmon all summer for winter use, they traveled into the

*The Dena'ina traditionally cremated their dead with the deceased person's weapons and tools for use in the afterlife. After Russian Orthodox priests prohibited cremation, Dena'ina people built shelters over loved ones' graves to hold their belongings. 1916. August Cohn Collection, Anchorage Museum.*

Chugach Mountains along the Eklutna River to hunt caribou, sheep, goats, bears and small game. (Moose weren't common in the Anchorage area until railroad builders burned its forests.) Since their fishing grounds were less plentiful than rivers belonging to the Dena'ina of Tyonek, on the west side of Cook Inlet, they traded hides, meat and sinew from their mountain hunting for fish. They also traded dried fish with the Ahtna up the Matanuska River in exchange for furs and meat.

Through winter most food came from caches where it was stored, both above ground on legs to protect the food from animals, and below ground to take advantage of the coolness of the earth. The leader of each nichił, called the qeshqa, directed the storage of food gathered by members of his house, managed trade with other villages, and dealt out the food during the hungry winter months. Intensive hunting happened in the winter only if supplies ran short. These were months for socializing and celebration: the Dena'ina word for November means "Visitors," for December, "Month we sing." The village waited until spring, when the salmon, eulachon and waterfowl returned and the cycle began again.

This cycle continued until the 1940s, when the rapid growth of the city of Anchorage, the necessity of formal schooling, and the taking of the land by newcomers cut off the ability to live off the land. The upper Cook Inlet Dena'ina had fended off every previous attempt to take their land or resources. Wars between tribes to capture slaves, seize goods and occupy territory happened long before white explorers arrived. Probably, the Dena'ina themselves took the upper Cook Inlet region from Eskimo people who lived there a millennium ago.

Shem Pete and other elders handed down the story of the last battle with the Aluutiq, which tradition puts in the mid 18th century. An Aluutiq raiding party brought eight skin boats over the Knik Glacier from Prince William Sound and down the Knik River. They encountered a newly married couple camping out along the river; the wife was captured, but the husband escaped and got word to leaders in Eklutna. Watching from one of the pair of hills that give the village its name, Eklutna people saw the Aluutiq trying to elude them, floating their disguised boats down Knik Arm. They pursued the raiders and caught the Aluutiq forces sleeping at Point Campbell. The Dena'ina killed the entire party, sparing just two boys who could return home to tell what had happened. The Aluutiq never attacked again.

But more formidable adversaries followed. Within decades of the battle with the Aluutiq, Dena'ina people saw two great, birdlike beasts approaching from the south, up the inlet. Two sailing ships were drifting northward on the tide into Dena'ina territory, rising up from the horizon as if emerging from the water. Each day of the passage up the coast the bravest Dena'ina men paddled out to the ships and tried to communicate and trade with the crews. The ships anchored near Ch'aghałnikt, the village on a point that extends north from the Kenai Peninsula toward the dividing of the inlet into its two arms near Anchorage.

Railroad crews arriving in 1915 slashed Ship Creek of timber and burned piles late into the night. This view looks south across the railroad camp from Government Hill. Courtesy of Mary Barry.

The two sides met on June 1, 1778. We know the story both from the oral tradition handed down by the Dena'ina and from logs kept by Captain James Cook and his officers. The British had been sent forth from Plymouth, England, to explore the Pacific Ocean and find a way around the north end of North America. Cook died the following February in Hawaii and the British admiralty named Cook Inlet for him - ironically, since the visit frustrated and disappointed him. Upon entering the inlet, the tides and geography convinced Cook it would not be the path to Europe, but he realized others would question his decision to sail onward if he didn't check it out. The two week side trip cost him precious time on his journey north.

Cook named Turnagain Arm for a maddening failed effort to explore it amidst contrary wind, currents and shoals. A boat sent up Knik Arm made it just far enough to see the lay of the land. Then Cook, anxious to leave, sent ashore Lt. James King and ship's surgeon James Law with two boats of men to claim the land for England. He named that place Point Possession.

The villagers of Ch'aghałnikt met them, first with weapons and wooden armor, and then, after all present showed they meant to be peaceful, putting down their weapons to drink beer with the visitors (it was English porter). They watched the sailors' strange ritual: taking some turf, hoisting a flag, and putting a scroll and some coins in an empty beer bottle and hiding it among some rocks. King, who had a sense of humor, noted, "if it escapes the Indians, in many ages hence it may Puzle Antiquarians."

The entire encounter puzzled the Dena'ina. They had no notion that by these simple acts the visitors somehow believed that they had taken ownership of the land. But they did get a strong sense of the Englishmen's power. Dr. Law traded for a dog from a Dena'ina man in exchange for two buckles. Then, when the dog jumped up, Law shot it in the head. The Dena'ina backed slowly away, and then ran, and could not be lured to return.

They remembered that senseless violence. The story, somewhat altered, came down through Shem Pete and other elders. In 1975, Feodoria Pennington said, "The small children of the village would always take a jar or can they found floating on the beach to Doris Nicolai to see if it was Captain Cook's."

Russian fur companies followed Cook into the region, but the Dena'ina resisted. Their war parties drove Russian settlements out of upper Cook Inlet, saving the Dena'ina from the fur-hunting slavery imposed on the brutally conquered people of the Aleutians, Kodiak Island and Prince William Sound. Instead, the Dena'ina hunted beaver for trade from their own lands and bought furs from tribes further inland to sell to the Russians. The area became a successful center of trade long before it was the city of Anchorage.

The Dena'ina people's health suffered as new germs invaded. A terrible epidemic killed many in the late 1830s. But the Dena'ina were

Tsat'ukegh, Shem Pete's home village, was also known as Susitna Station. It was a thriving Susitna River way station at the time of this photograph, in 1917, but the village later depopulated. Photo by P. S. Hunt, Alaska Railroad Collection, Anchorage Museum.

The old was erased so rapidly and completely that today a leader of the Dena'ina in Anchorage, Eklutna Tribal Council President Lee Stephan, calls on fragmentary memories and old photographs to bring back a sense of what his village's past was like. For the city's centennial the Anchorage Museum mounted an exhibit on the Dena'ina that brought together materials and interpretation never gathered together before. Stephan gave a welcome, but could not do so in his people's own language.

"I'm kind of disappointed I have to find out about me in a museum," Stephan said later. "All the stuff I should have learned, I could have learned, I wanted to learn, and nobody teach me. I had to find it in a museum. We call Jim Fall and Jim Kari the fathers of our language. They speak fluently to me Athabascan, and I don't have any concept of what they say at all." (Fall says he is not fluent, although Kari is.)

The memories of Shem Pete were once again given life in the exhibit. Jim Fall helped translate them into physical reality with other anthropologists and curators. The galleries opened with a full-sized model of a fish camp like the ones that once stood along the shore of Anchorage, lifelike except that the scene was perfectly still and free of the fragrant odors of a real stream bank. The only Dena'ina fishing site left in Anchorage is shared by the fifty residents of Eklutna under an educational permit granted by the State of Alaska with a severe limit on the number of fish they can catch. Stephan gets most of his fish as other Anchorage residents do: with a rod and reel.

Eklutna is the size of a single cul-de-sac in a typical Anchorage subdivision. Modest homes have toys and swingsets outside, surrounded by acres of wooded land. The sound of cars on the four-lane Glenn Highway is rarely absent, and trains and a pipeline run through the village.

A Russian Orthodox Church built by missionaries, the oldest building in the region, stands near the famous Eklutna cemetery, where

prosperous and still controlled their own communities when American gold rush prospectors arrived in the 1890s. In 1896, an explorer visiting Shem's birthplace, Susitna Station, found the residents, "industrious, … thrifty and foresighted." Their way of life remained mostly intact, as hunters and as traders. The Alaska Commercial Company had a trading post in the village, but so did Shem's brother, who died rich and respected by both races. Travelers jumped off there on trips to the Interior.

But in the days from 1914 to the present, those patterns of trade disappeared and Anchorage came into being, a new trade center for Alaska and a transportation crossroads for the region and eventually for the hemisphere.

each grave has a brightly painted cover the size of a large doll house. The Dena'ina traditionally cremated their dead with the weapons and tools they would need in the afterlife. When missionary priests prohibited cremation, they began building these grave houses to give the spirits of their loved ones a home to keep their necessary belongings before they could move onward. When tourists got interested in the cemetery, villagers began maintaining the houses and decorating them. In the old days, they were simple structures designed to decay as time passed and the spirits passed to the next world.

Most of the change came this way, through steps of adaptation to the outsiders rather than in the kind of battles in which the Dena'ina had held the world at bay before 1914. Newcomers pushed them out simply by taking their land and fish camps and using the sites for something else.

The ancient site of Tak'at, just north of the Port of Anchorage, had a log platform that allowed fishermen to dip through the tidal cycle. Long before Shem Pete's time it had been a major gathering place, rich in fish, and even had a nichił winter house. Rufe and Annie Stephan hosted the last Dena'ina potlatch there around 1930. The celebration lasted through three days of eating, singing and drumming on a seven-foot-long plank (the Dena'ina didn't use skin drums in those days). But a few years later the military burned the smokehouse and began dumping garbage at the site. The Stephan family started fishing on Montana Creek instead.

The Dena'ina lost memories the same way they lost land: new people simply pushed tradition aside. Rather than learning to hunt and do other subsistence work, Lee Stephan attended Chugiak High School. He should have graduated in 1973, but he skipped class to hide in the woods, avoiding lessons that seemed irrelevant. His mother and father had attended a Bureau of Indian Affairs school where their mouths were washed out with soap for repeating Dena'ina stories.

*Bald eagle and chick, Potter Marsh, 2005. Photo by Bob Hallinen, copyright Alaska Dispatch News.*

But today, Lee Stephan is a cheerful and enthusiastic leader. The village has many plans. Thanks to the 1971 Alaska Native Claims Settlement Act, the Eklutna Corp. is the largest land owner in Anchorage. Most of that land isn't available for use in the traditional ways. Anchorage has greenbelts and bike trails instead of fish camps. But the Eklutna people can reap income and a prosperous future from Alaska's largest city.

The Dena'ina are still here. Not erased, but woven into Anchorage. It happened much as a shaman from Susitna Station predicted. This was among Shem Pete's favorite stories, the shaman of his home village, then called Tsat'ukegh, foretelling the great flu epidemic of 1918 and the influx of non-Natives.

"He told us, 'I see nothing left from that sickness come. You people just like burn the grass down," Shem recalled. " 'Pretty soon gonna be something happen. Listen carefully,' he said. 'There gonna be white man gonna be just like this sand.' He pick it up in his hand, the sand. 'You fellows gonna be not living one place. Few here, few there, all over just scattered along like little berries between them white people.'"

Five years after leaving for the Klondike Gold Rush in 1897, Will Langille came home to Oregon with a lot of ideas about how Alaska should be protected from greedy exploitation, but not gold. He had been among the first of the gold rush over the Chilkoot Pass, mushed the breadth of Alaska with a four-dog team, and spent months at a time prospecting around Nome without so much as a blanket to keep warm. His solo travels mark him as one of the greatest outdoorsmen of Alaska history. But the ideas he brought home were more important than the adventure stories. They helped shape Alaska and the huge political controversy that helped bring Anchorage into existence.

# *Chapter 2*

## *Will Langille:*
## *Scandal and the Railroad Route*

*Will Langille about 1885, before he left Oregon for the Klondike Gold Rush. Moody-McKeown Collection, Oregon Historical Society.*

Langille was the son of a single mother and quit school after the eighth grade. He spent his youth climbing Mt. Hood, in Oregon, with his younger brother, Doug, and exploring the surrounding wilderness, learning everything he could about the plants and trees there. When his mother Sarah took over running the Cloud Cap Inn, high on the mountain, Will and Doug became climbing guides for the guests. Her hospitality, their skill, and the spectacular setting gave the inn a reputation that brought important people from all over the United States. Will and Doug learned from the visitors and passed on their knowledge, making connections and trading information with top scientists and politicians who were then reconsidering how America should use its land and natural resources.

A pair of guests in August 1901 pulled the Langille boys deeply into that debate. Teddy Roosevelt had recently become vice president. His close friend and boxing and tennis partner Gifford Pinchot heard about Cloud Cap Inn and decided to visit while traveling with Frederick Newell, another member of Roosevelt's circle of influential, conservation-minded friends. Will was off in Alaska, but Doug hauled the visitors on an exhausting two-day trek, taught them about the area, and showed how it was being damaged by sheep grazing and fires. It lacked proper land management.

A month later President William McKinley was assassinated and Roosevelt became president. Roosevelt put Pinchot in charge of his conservation agenda and Pinchot brought Doug Langille to Washington, D.C., to help manage the nation's forests and create the U.S. Forest Service.

Will Langille wrote home from Alaska. The nature there fascinated him and the beauty affected him. His vivid letters show him to be capable, daring and honest, and impatient with people lacking those qualities. A work supervisor found him "mildly terrifying." Word

*Clouds at Potter Marsh, 2012. Photo by Bob Hallinen, copyright* Anchorage Dispatch News.

spread of how he made friends with legendary pioneer tough-guy Jack Dalton by facing him down without flinching when Dalton pulled a gun. Physically Will was tall, strong and had great posture. His adversaries respected him.

Will took in stride the winter that Jack London turned into harrowing stories of gold rush hardship. Of camping out at - 44 degrees Fahrenheit, he wrote to his mother, "To you I suppose it seems like something terrible to be sleeping out on the snow with the 'quick' down that low, but we had plenty of blankets and kept warm, the worst thing cooking, the dough freezes before you can get it all kneaded, and everything of metal sticks to your fingers."

Will's letters tell funny stories and adventures, describe plant samples he was sending along, and shared with Doug his ideas about conserving Alaska. The place had value for the long term, for development that would support the people and wildlife permanently. But instead get-rich-quick scammers were robbing the future and each other for anything they could take away. He ultimately came to believe all of Alaska should be managed with conservation and sustained use in mind, for its own benefit.

Pinchot read the letters. Soon after Will returned to Oregon, Pinchot asked him to come to Washington, and then sent him back to Alaska, this time as a federal employee. Through 1903 and 1904 he explored on his own by rowboat, power launch, on foot, on horseback, behind a dog sled and on snowshoes, covering Southeast Alaska, the coast from Yakutat to Kodiak, including Prince William Sound, and Cook Inlet. He investigated the Seward Peninsula around Nome, and went into the Interior, the Tanana River Valley, the Susitna Valley, the Copper River country, and many other places—including the area we know as the Anchorage bowl.

Alaska was up for grabs. Laws made in the 1800s created a system to give private parties access to public resources by filing claims on resources such as gold, oil or coal, timber or rock. The huge gold discoveries in 1897 and 1898, all of them near Canada's Klondike River, had set off a rush of tens of thousands of Americans seeking to get rich by filing gold claims, among them Will Langille. The flood of greedy newcomers then spread across a territory they regarded as free land (few recognized the ownership rights of Alaska Natives), and created a rich hunting ground for swindlers and con men.

Frauds targeted gold rushers and the government. Phony gold mines, fake towns, and imaginary railroads were announced and even partially built, all to trick investors into buying worthless property deeds or stock. Frauds against the government focused on getting around laws intended to limit how much government land or resources one person could take. Companies and speculators would organize groups to individually file on claims and then transfer them to a single owner, who could then tie up huge deposits of minerals for little cost.

Will later wrote to his superiors: "Since 1898 Alaska has been cursed with unscrupulous promoters and their visionary 'get rich quick' schemes, who have elaborated upon and magnified every mineral discovery and every possible resource, until it was conceived to be a land where wealth was to be had with little or no effort. Glowing prospectuses have deceived large investors and coaxed from their hiding places the savings of the poor, to be wasted in some unfeasible and fruitless endeavors from which it was never possible to receive returns."

The wildest frenzy of speculation, fraud and swindling exploded around the Kennicott copper find in the Wrangell Mountains, the richest in the world, owned by the Alaska Syndicate, an investment group of America's wealthiest families: J.P. Morgan and the Guggenheims. Getting the copper out would require building a 200-mile railroad from the mountains to the sea, with towns and docks to connect the trains to shipping. The railroad would also need coal to power the locomotives.

Claims for coal, oil and railroad rights-of-way blanketed the wilderness coast from the Bering River to eastern Prince William Sound. Some of the proposed railroads were obviously impossible to build, requiring massive trestles across miles of stormy waters. Three lines were planned in and around the shifting sands and ferocious winds of Controller Bay, near the brand-new town of Katalla. A storm swept away an expensive harbor breakwater in its first winter. Will found $100 million in stock had been issued for various railroads at Katalla and Controller Bay (worth about $2 billion in today's dollars).

Railroad workers tried to build track to Kennecott from competing towns. In Keystone Canyon, near Valdez, a gun fight broke out over access to a route. In Katalla, competing railroaders blew up each other's track and opposing work crews fought battles with clubs. One side dipped their clubs in black pitch so they could tell friend from foe. Money flowed and chaos reigned.

Based on Will's reports, Gifford Pinchot drafted an executive order for President Roosevelt to create the Chugach National Forest and greatly expand the Tongass National Forest (they were then called forest reserves), which the president signed in 1907. The Chugach spread over almost the entire Kenai Peninsula and all of what is now known as Anchorage, north to the Knik River, plus Prince William Sound and eastward, beyond the Copper River into the mountains around the Bering River, including the area coveted by the railroad builders. Roosevelt also froze all coal claims in Alaska, allowing none to be filed until Congress could pass a law to require miners to pay the government for the coal.

Pinchot put Will in charge of the new forest reserves and he bore the brunt of the fury of Alaskans who believed the conservationists were destroying their chances for Alaska riches (that was when Dalton pulled the gun on him). Pinchot was burned in effigy in Katalla. In Cordova, residents threw a load of imported coal off the dock, like the Boston Tea Party. National media reported these events. It was an unusual moment in history, when a very popular president put his unprecedented power behind the dreams of an idealist, Gifford Pinchot, and an indignant nature lover alone on the frontier, Will Langille.

The moment didn't last. In 1909, Roosevelt left the presidency and departed for a long African safari. Before he moved out of the White House he extracted an agreement from his successor, William Howard Taft, to keep Pinchot in charge of conservation. Taft and Roosevelt were close friends and Roosevelt had chosen Taft to follow him in the presidency. But Taft was more cautious and conservative than Roosevelt and he didn't trust Pinchot. He put a different kind of reformer in charge of public lands: Interior Secretary Richard Ballinger, a lawyer and a former mayor of Seattle.

Before Anchorage, the village of Knik, on the far side of Knik Arm, was the area's commercial center. With these 1912 postcards, the Knik Commercial Club tried to attract investment and new residents. Pratt Collection, Anchorage Museum.

Under Roosevelt, Ballinger had cleaned up the General Land Office, the agency responsible for mining claims and homesteads. He fired lazy or corrupt workers and put honest men in their jobs. Unlike Pinchot, who was born rich and devoted his education and life to his ideals, Ballinger was a self-made man, a pro-development westerner with a practical outlook. He wanted development to happen, but honestly.

Pinchot remained in charge of the Forest Service, but with much less influence. Feeling helpless while, he believed, Taft was reversing

Roosevelt's conservation policies, he fought bitterly with Ballinger. When a whistleblower in the land office brought him evidence that Ballinger had approved fraudulent coal claims for the Alaska Syndicate on the Bering River, he blew up the issue into a national scandal that forced Taft to choose between the two of them. Taft fired Pinchot and Congressional hearings were called to look into the Ballinger-Pinchot Affair.

The coal claims had been organized by Clarence Cunningham, who recruited a variety of false applicants to put together a sizable coal mining area for the Alaska Syndicate. Ballinger never benefited personally by approving the claims over the objections of his land office inspector. He probably thought he was doing right, as that was the only way to get coal for trains to Kennecott in the face of an unworkable law.

The Forest Service sent Will Langille with a team to trek into the mountains up the Bering River and investigate the Cunningham Claims. The area, then as now, was wild and tough to get to. The General Land Office dispatched a young lawyer from the new crop of men brought in by Ballinger to handle the issue in an Alaska office: he was Andrew Christensen, later to be one of the founders and early leaders of Anchorage.

But the issue became much bigger than these individuals or any Alaska coal. The Congressional hearings made front-page news daily, a court of public opinion to choose between two men and two philosophies. President Taft's allies had wanted the hearings to regain the political initiative over Pinchot, thinking they could expose his insubordination and insider maneuvering. But Pinchot had as his lawyer Louis Brandeis, who would later become one of the nation's greatest Supreme Court Justices. Brandeis crushed his opponents. He proved that Taft himself had lied to cover for Ballinger by back-dating a key document and by claiming authorship of a letter exonerating Ballinger that Ballinger himself had written.

Roosevelt heard about all this with dismay when he returned from his safari. Pinchot traveled to Italy under an alias to meet him as soon as he arrived from Africa. They talked in Roosevelt's hotel room all day and until late at night—about Taft's supposed betrayal. The controversy would become a major reason why Roosevelt and Taft ended their friendship, with Roosevelt preparing to run against Taft in the 1912 election.

What was this fight really about? Alaska to that point had produced plenty of gold and fish, but nothing to justify the intensity of the conflict in Washington. Will Langille had urged caution in estimating the value of Alaska's resources. The costs and barriers for development were huge. But that truth didn't fit the political story of the day.

*Steam locomotives were the power behind construction of railroads during the era, and the first mechanized mode of ground transportation in Alaska. Courtesy of Todd Hardesty.*

Development promoters, during the gold rush as today, can exaggerate resource opportunities to push their projects, until they start to believe their own propaganda. The political adversaries of the Ballinger-Pinchot Affair got carried away as well. To justify his position, Pinchot asserted in the *Saturday Evening Post* that the coal deposit was large enough to power the entire U.S. West Coast for 20 years. On their side, Ballinger's backers said the conservationists were destroying the opportunity for construction of great foundries, factories, railroads and cities in Alaska.

After the hearings, Pinchot and a few others went to see for themselves, and learned, like Langille, that the coal on the Cunningham Claims was low in quality and expensive to access. It never would be developed. The port at Katalla was impractical and storm-battered. The Alaska Syndicate instead reached its Kennecott mine from Cordova via the Copper River and Northwestern Railway, which ran on oil, not coal.

Katalla, once the center of a national controversy, was eventually abandoned and is now overgrown with forest. Unfinished railbeds still trace through the woods. A stranded steam locomotive rusts away.

Despite reality, however, the belief had been planted deeply in the public imagination that the only thing blocking limitless wealth coming from Alaska was a lack of honesty and competence in Washington. The issue did not die after Ballinger resigned and the Cunningham claims were cancelled. A fistfight broke out on the floor of the U.S. House over a coal leasing bill for Alaska. Taft remained on the defensive. In a special message to Congress in 1911 he acknowledged the failure to open up Alaska, but tried to deflect blame. He said, "If the development of Alaska has been retarded, it is those scandalmongers, who raise the cry of 'fraud' and 'grab' whenever any action is taken by the administration affecting Alaska, who are alone responsible."

*Violent battles erupted between railroad construction crews competing to reach mines from Katalla and other coastal towns, here in 1907. Only one line succeeded, from Cordova to the copper mine at Kennicott, until the federal government built the Alaska Railroad, partly to counter that 'monopoly.' Photo by J.C. Evans, CIHS Reeve Collection, Anchorage Museum.*

All Alaska boosters agreed that a railroad to the Interior would be the key to unlock the territory's fabulous wealth. In 1912, Taft got Congress to fund an Alaska Railroad Commission to study the best route for a government-built railroad—a unique initiative in American history. The commission looked particularly at two options to get from the ocean to Fairbanks. A new line could start at Chitina, already served from Cordova by the Copper River and Northwestern Railway, with 313 miles of new track generally following the route of today's Richardson Highway. That was the Eastern Route. The other likely option would start from Seward, run around the head of Cook Inlet, up the Susitna River and through the Alaska Range at Broad Pass. It was called the Western Route. Building from the end of a ramshackle, partly completed railroad from Seward to Turnagain Arm, called the Alaska Northern, the Western Route would require 391 miles of new rail to get to Fairbanks.

The hardest part of the Eastern Route had already been built, from Cordova up the Copper River to Chitina, which the government could buy from the Alaska Syndicate or simply connect to. Taking that into account, the commission concluded that a railway to Fairbanks by the Eastern Route would be less expensive, easier to build, and would carry more tonnage of freight, giving the government's line a better chance to be a money-maker.

But by the time the commission delivered its report, Taft had already lost the 1912 election (he came in third, after Democrat Woodrow Wilson and Roosevelt, who ran under the banner of his own Bull Moose Party). The commission report became a political problem for the incoming president. He wanted to build a railroad, but he did not want to do business with the Alaska Syndicate.

In his first State of the Union Address, in December, 1913, Wilson said, "Alaska, as a storehouse, should be unlocked. One key to it is a system of railways." Legislation to fund a railroad was already working its way through Congress. Advocates predicted a government-owned railroad opening a farming and mining boom in Alaska, bringing a rush of new settlement, and breaking the strangle hold of the Alaska Syndicate on the boundless wealth of the north. Alaska's non-voting congressional delegate, James Wickersham, gave a brilliant four-hour floor speech in which he vilified the Morgan-Guggenheim partnership. He said, "When people inquire what is wrong with Alaska it may be answered: The Alaska Syndicate."

The bill that passed authorized $35 million for a project which would ultimately cost $72 million. To give a sense of the enormous scale, the federal government spent only $735 million on everything that year. The United States would build a railroad into the wilderness, the first and only railroad it ever built, for a cost equivalent of nearly 10 percent of all federal spending for a year.

Explaining such an extraordinary decision requires the context of the times. The Progressive Movement, which rose in response to the excesses of unrestrained capitalism in the Nineteenth Century, reached its greatest strength with the presidencies of Roosevelt and Wilson. Progressives believed in a strong, activist government as the counterweight to corporate power in society. They broke up and regulated monopolies and advocated for government ownership of utilities and railroads. Roosevelt's triumphant project to build and operate the Panama Canal reflected progressive ideals and the Alaska Railroad became the canal's natural follow-up. Its builders even used hand-me-down equipment from the Canal Zone.

President Wilson signed the railroad bill in March 1914. The legislation put decisions about building the railroad in his hands, including the route. He would not choose the Eastern Route, despite its advantages, because that would mean buying the Copper River and

Northwestern Railway from the Alaska Syndicate for $18 million. Wilson had become president partly because he was a progressive who opposed monopolies, and the Ballinger-Pinchot Affair had made the Alaska Syndicate infamous. Wilson sent another commission to Alaska, supposedly to take a more careful look, but it barely considered the Eastern Route. Instead, the new commission planned a railroad from Seward and through the site of the future Anchorage. When Wilson announced his selection in April 1915, the decision had long been made.

While politics dictated Wilson would pick the Western Route, the flat land at Ship Creek was a real advantage for the railroad. The March 1914 bill that funded the railroad set aside a three-mile-square reserve in the Chugach National Forest for a terminal and town there. With plenty of buildable ground and a safe anchorage for ships, this could be a port for shipment of material into Alaska to build the railroad, and for exporting coal from the Matanuska Valley.

But the entire area that would become Anchorage remained part of Chugach National Forest, even the small railroad reserve. Forest Service officials who studied it believed that it should remain part of the forest, based on the findings and philosophy originally laid out by Will Langille. Promoters of the railroad and of the towns it would serve wanted to do away with the national forest entirely, but consistently failed.

Will himself missed that fight. He moved on to new adventures in South America, leaving behind a report in 1911 that called on the government to include the entire territory of Alaska under the control of the Forest Service. His Forest Service career had been spent fighting fraud and unrealistic expectations about Alaska resources. He had come to see the value of complete ecosystems for conservation and believed that development should continue slowly and carefully within the bounds of the natural system.

"After six years of private life followed by eight years in connection with Government forest work in Alaska, there can be but one conclusion as to the advisability of retaining in the Government the title to the forest lands of that region," he wrote. "Conservation is, to some extent, delaying development, but not actually injuring Alaska. It is hurting the speculators who cry out against it. It is giving the people a chance to consider its possibilities, and ultimately legitimate investments will be made and judiciously expended in the development of Alaska's real resources, which are of worth, and the growth of empire will go on slowly but steadily, and not the least of these resources are the forests which it is great wisdom to retain in the care of the Forest Service."

In 1915, the first tracks of the Alaska Railroad led from the landing at Ship Creek to buildings and tents erected in the terminal yard by the Alaska Engineering Commission. Photo by Sydney Laurence, Pyatt-Laurence Collection, Anchorage Museum.

# Chapter 3

## Andrew Christensen: Building a Government Town

THE OPENING OF THE AUCTION SALE OF LOTS AT ANCHORAGE ALASK
BY THE U.S. GOVT FIRST LOT SOLD FOR 825

*Andrew Christensen presiding over the first Anchorage townsite auction, July 10, 1915. Courtesy of Todd Hardesty.*

At the end of 1915 Anchorage was less than six months old, but already had 1,500 year-round residents, a school with 150 students, a filtered water system, a phone line to Seward, a government amusement hall, and a rail line reaching as far as Eagle River. Development had been rapid and orderly, with every aspect under the control of the federal government, through the Interior Department's General Land Office, the railroad-building Alaskan Engineering Commission, and the U.S. Forest Service, among other agencies. The Commission published a year-end report that declared, with ill-concealed pride, "It is felt that the Government is to be congratulated on the success of its first experiment in town building in Alaska."

The author of those words is unknown—government reports are impersonal—but the voice is likely that of Andrew Christensen, an eager and imaginative bureaucrat who is, as much as anyone, the city's father. Thanks to Christensen we know extraordinary detail about Anchorage's early days. He excelled in his work and submitted periodic reports on his progress that ran beyond 100 pages, with only an assistant and a stenographer to help him. They detail his efforts to build and manage the railroad towns of Anchorage, Wasilla, Matanuska, Eska and Nenana, while also stimulating the agriculture and industry of Alaska. The reports are boastful, argumentative, and crammed with recommendations and ideas, from the mundane to the impractical. About Christensen personally we know little. The record tells only of his job. But he obviously loved his job.

A westerner, Christensen had worked in railroading before getting a law degree and moving to Washington, D.C. In 1908, he joined Richard Ballinger's reforming General Land Office, proved his skill, and the next year went to Alaska, taking over the critical job of managing the Alaska coal claims that became a national scandal in the fight between Ballinger and Gifford Pinchot, the founder of the Forest Service.

He was a mirror image of the competent and energetic Forest Service conservationists: similar, but with a reversed point of view. He worked as hard as they did, wrote as persuasively, and believed as strongly, but he thought their ideas about reserving vast Alaskan resources were ridiculous. He dreamed instead of a frontier spawning great cities, farms, mines and industrial plants like those of the American West.

In 1918, Christensen wrote, "The question is frequently asked, 'Will the railroad pay?' The same question was asked about the Union and Central Pacific, the Northern Pacific and other transcontinental railroads. Duluth was held up to ridicule in Congress. It is presumed that those who criticized so freely then, would, if they were alive, deny that they ever had any doubts about the investment! There is no reason to doubt that someday—and it may be sooner than expected—the Alaska Railroad will also be a paying investment."

The Chugach National Forest outraged Christensen and many Alaskans as a barrier to the territory's prosperous future. Alaska's congressional delegate, Wickersham, called for abolishing the Chugach entirely in 1911. When the Territorial Legislature convened for the first time in 1913, one of its initial actions was to pass a resolution demanding the Chugach be eliminated and its lands opened to development. The war between the developers at the Interior Department and the land conservationists at the Forest Service continued for years to come.

U.S. Forest Service Guard Jack Brown in his tent-office at the mouth of Ship Creek, 1912. Jack and his wife Nellie would become residents of Anchorage when it came into existence three years later, covering lands Jack had explored. Photograph by Nellie Brown, courtesy of Mary Barry.

The front line of this war centered around Ship Creek, the future site of Anchorage, which lay entirely within the Chugach National Forest. The Forest Service dispatched a Scotsman hired as a forest guard by Will Langille to set up a ranger station there in 1912. Jack Brown and his Eyak Indian wife Nellie lived at first in a tent, then

*Main Street in the tent city near Ship Creek, 1915. Businessmen set up shop without owning the land, gold-rush style, before moving their operations to newly divided lots sold by the government on the bluff above the creek. Photo by Sydney Laurence, courtesy of Mary Barry*

moved into a log cabin next to the creek's mouth. Jack tramped around the area, exploring Ship Creek, Campbell Creek, Fish Creek, Point Woronzof, Point Campbell, and Eklutna Lake, and writing reports back to Washington about what he found.

Brown worked with Christensen, too, prosecuting a theft of timber by a homesteader in the thick forests of Girdwood in 1914. As absurd as the case may have seemed to Christensen, he was a lawyer and bureaucrat first, vigorously enforcing the law even where timber was abundant and just getting to the site of the alleged theft was an adventure. While traveling from Ship Creek to Girdwood to serve Christensen's subpoena on one Axel Lindblad, a witness, Brown's boat was driven on the beach near Hope and hopelessly stuck. The whole trip took eight days and when he arrived, Lindblad wasn't at home. Brown had to go back again the next week.

Smart observers could see that the Ship Creek area would be key to construction of a government railroad. The speed at which officials selected

the site is evidence of that. President Wilson took office in March, 1913, and made the railroad a major priority in December. The railroad bill passed in March 1914, and less than three months later, in June, a party of five men with 20 horses and supplies of lumber and equipment arrived at Ship Creek aboard the steamship *Dirigo* to set up a headquarters for eleven survey parties assigned to pick the railroad's route.

With local help, the Alaskan Engineering Commission, known as the AEC, built offices and corrals by the creek. Supposedly the president hadn't selected a route yet, but the massive surveying project concentrated on the Western Route. They tracked the Ship Creek weather—1914 was a lovely summer—and hired an observer to watch how much ice floated by in the winter. The AEC engaged a marine navigation expert, R.S. Patton, to verify that the port could serve as a gateway to Alaska. He reported, "If a railroad is built, it will follow the south shore of Knik Arm and … Ship Creek will be one of the most important tide water points on the line—certainly for the construction and very possibly as a permanent shipping point as well."

The rush for resource wealth had spawned other towns in Alaska. Usually a gold find came first, followed by men who hoped to get rich quickly, and the men and women who made money off of them, through alcohol sales, prostitution, gambling and fraud. Boomtowns were chaotic, filthy and dangerous. Saloons and brothels came before police or clean water. Men were robbed, shot and cut down by epidemics. Order came later, after the rush, when the boomtown would be abandoned or live on with whatever industry local resources could sustainably support.

The progressive federal officials who founded Anchorage had a different plan. Development happened in a rush, as in a gold rush. But here there was no resource to exploit, and the selection of the site was made by experts who carefully studied the geography and engineering challenges, guided by the political realities, and with the full force of the presidency behind them. Given the facts at hand, the flat land around Ship Creek made sense as a headquarters and transportation center. With the extraordinary support of Congress and the taxpayers, the government skipped the normal process through which a population center normally develops and simply installed a town.

While AEC crews surveyed and staked the route of the railroad, Jack Brown marked the boundaries of a three-by-three-mile railroad townsite that had been set aside near Ship Creek. But the work went no further. The government hadn't built a town before and no one had decided even who would be in charge. The land remained part of Chugach National Forest and its officials believed Brown was responsible for it as the forest guard. But the General Land Office had told Christensen he was in charge.

The personalities of the two men made a difference. Brown went on exploring and investigating as a forest guard. But Christensen understood that people were coming and pleaded with his superiors in November, 1914, to allow him to lay out a town and prepare to sell private property along its streets. They did not respond. In the meantime, Brown quit his job to make money running supply boats in the coming boom.

The AEC delivered its survey report to the president February 22, 1915. It didn't recommend a route, but the intent to build the Western Route was obvious. Five days later, the commission sent the Secretary of the Interior a scope of work to construct the route and dredge the harbor at "Ship Creek Junction," and requested

Mudflats and large tides made the mouth of Ship Creek a difficult place to land. This photograph was taken the same month the Alaska Engineering Commission arrived with the first load of supplies to build the Alaska Railroad and the new city. Photograph by Sydney Laurence. Muller Collection, Anchorage Museum.

*Andrew Christensen optimistically laid out wide streets for the new town of Anchorage, which initially had little traffic other than pedestrians. Shown here, Fourth Avenue in 1915. Courtesy of Mary Barry.*

Restaurants, clothiers, a billiard hall and many one-room brothels occupied canvas tents set up on the muddy ground near the creek. Mears hired as many men as he could for immediate work—a crew of 100 at $3 for an eight-hour day—but hundreds more disembarked with each ship, and within weeks 2,000 people were living in the tents and shacks, paying 5 cents a bucket for drinking water and going to the bathroom wherever they could find a spot.

This was not the orderly railroad town the engineers had contemplated, and it lay directly atop the ground Mears needed to build the yards and terminal. The commission's surgeon warned of water contamination due to the lack of sanitation. Moreover, railroad builders worried of riots and labor unrest. The men wanted work quickly and at higher pay than the railroad offered.

Christensen worried especially about many arrivals who were immigrants with limited English. Officials discussed bringing in troops to assure order. Christensen wrote a letter to the Forest Service demanding it evict everyone; this may have been a trap, as to attempt it would have been a disaster, and the forest supervisor wisely ignored the letter. Mears instead urged the land office to quickly carry out Christensen's plan to set up a proper town on the bluff south of Ship Creek.

The townspeople and AEC were impatient, but action came lightning fast by federal government standards. By May 6, Christensen had permission to lay out the town. Making decisions on the fly with Mears, he cleared paths through the wooded land on a plateau south of the creek, the area we know as downtown Anchorage, following the imaginary routes of wide, straight streets marked and named on a map with letters and numbers. The grid pattern made for steep grades up the bluff, so a curving road climbed from the creek bottom. It was named Christensen Drive.

funds to get started. Lieutenant Frederick Mears, the commission member in charge of actual construction, went to Seattle to buy materials. When President Wilson formally announced his selection of the Western Route on April 10, Mears was ready and set sail eight days later with equipment to build a dock and storage yard at Ship Creek and supplies to begin clearing the route toward the Matanuska Valley.

When Mears arrived on April 26, he found a tent city already established on the flatlands around the creek. Anyone reading the newspapers had been able to see money would be made at Ship Creek, and money powered the churn of Alaska's itinerant population. The territory had been gold rushing for two decades. Its roaming workers, entrepreneurs, bootleggers and flim-flam men were experts at installing instant boomtowns.

Christensen believed in the wisdom of government, just as the Forest Service conservationists did. The rules governing the sale of lots in the new town, rapidly issued over President Wilson's signature, established a community in which the federal government retained management, responsibility and even control of private property. The lots would be sold at auction, but buyers wouldn't receive title for five years, and even then the deeds could only be issued to the original bidder, complicating land sales. If a buyer used the property for immoral purposes, such as drinking, gambling or prostitution, the government could take it back. Banks wouldn't lend based on the restrictions, taxes couldn't be levied, nor a local government established. The federal government would have to oversee every aspect of civic life.

The auction of lots on July 10, 1915, is often regarded as the event that founded the city. Christensen stood on a platform before a crowd of bidders in the tent city and gave a stirring speech about the future. When the bidding began, money flowed with abandon. The new town was a smashing success. (Jack and Nellie Brown bought a lot on L Street, where they established the first pumped well.) Over the next month the creek bottom cleared. Residents and businessmen dragged their buildings and tents behind teams of horses up the bluff to their new lots.

Steve McCutcheon arrived that summer on his fourth birthday. He told the story of his family finding its lot at C Street and Seventh Avenue, although if he could really remember that walk he was not sure. "In any event, I remember the conversation, at least, about when we came up C Street," he said, in the 1990s. "There were still stumps in the way there. It wasn't a street yet. It was just a trail. ... The first winter of 1915-16, we lived in a tent. During that winter, why, my dad and our neighbor, a guy by the name of Smith Higgins, cut the logs off our property and some of the properties just behind and built a house."

The Alaska Engineering Commission imported supplies and began building warehouses in the spring of 1915, working with horse teams and locomotives on new rails. Photo by Sydney Laurence. Courtesy of Mary Barry.

The AEC and General Land Office ran everything. Christensen and the AEC commissioners received advice from the Anchorage Chamber of Commerce, formed by business owners in the city's first year, but the locals' feelings didn't always carry weight. For example, the townspeople voted in August 1915 to name the community "Alaska City," but federal officials picked "Anchorage" instead because the post office was already using that name.

Townspeople constantly complained, but they wanted to keep this odd form of local government that gave services without taxes. The Chamber of Commerce asked the AEC to prevent private industry from setting up power and phone systems. The businessmen wanted the AEC to build and operate the utilities and schools as they had already done with the infirmary, fire department and roads. They expected government-owned utilities to charge lower rates than private, for-profit businesses.

*Anchorage residents resisted forming a town government until 1920, preferring federal management without local taxes. The Anchorage Chamber of Commerce, shown here in 1916, provided the only effective voice for residents, as it advised the federal Alaska Engineering Commission. Photo by P. S. Hunt. Alaska Railroad Collection, Anchorage Museum.*

Christensen ran the town first through the land office and then as head of the AEC's Land and Industrial Department. His most difficult early challenge was controlling vice and organized crime. Anchorage rocked and rolled like any gold rush boomtown, with high stakes gambling and wide-open drinking, although card rooms and saloons were theoretically outlawed. Scores of prostitutes worked from squalid tents and shacks called cribs, all controlled by pimps and a corrupt deputy U.S. Marshal.

According to Christensen's reports, the deputy owned the property where the most notorious gambling house stood and he lived, unmarried, with a woman bootlegger. Rather than clean things up, the deputy used his authority to skim gambling profits and control the prostitutes. He threatened the women with arrest or expulsion from Alaska if they didn't do as they were told, pay what was demanded of them, and stay in the area designated as the red light district.

The situation embarrassed the AEC, but Mears concentrated on building the railroad and would not get involved. Christensen did his best. The land law gave him the authority to seize property used for immoral purposes, but that process was long and complicated. To get around the corrupt police, he led his own raid on a pool hall called "The Bank" and swept up fourteen gamblers. But the deputy marshal managed to rig the trial jury and, despite overwhelming evidence, all were acquitted.

Authorities and community leaders believed prostitution was a necessity in a frontier community full of single working men to keep proper women safe. But the townsite rules gave Christensen no place to put them—prostitutes were barred from even bidding at the government's land auctions. Ingeniously, he used the predicament to inflict pain on his enemy, the Forest Service.

Christensen waited until Forest Service deputy supervisor T.M. Hunt left town, shortly before the townsite auction, then quickly built a road to just beyond the AEC's boundary, where Chugach National Forest controlled the land and was establishing a campground for transient workers. With help from the deputy marshal, Christensen moved the women and their cribs to the site. The new red light district, at the southeast corner of Ninth Avenue and C Street, was nicknamed "Huntsville," after the forest supervisor.

Hunt got back to town in time to see the feverish haste of the prostitutes' move still in progress. He confronted Christensen, who admitted he had "caught him with the goods," but didn't offer any solution other than to send an AEC doctor to check the women periodically.

Henry Solon Graves, the national head of the Forest Service, was already on his way to Anchorage. After so many calls to abolish the Chugach National Forest, he came to see the situation for himself. Arriving in Anchorage on September 2, 1915 he was not impressed.

"Mud was everywhere," he wrote in his diary. "The streets are being cleared after the houses put up for business. Great piles of refuse still in the streets. Quantities of men moving about through the streets, planning, looking at lots, speculating. There are enough merchant houses and restaurants for a town four times the size.

"In afternoon we went over to look at the public camp ground. I made up my mind to put a stop to it."

But despite Graves' fury, Christensen refused to move the prostitutes. The war between the agencies continued. Christensen believed Anchorage was being stifled by the surrounding Chugach National Forest. In March 1916, he attended a meeting in Washington, D.C., to present his views on abolishing the national forest. The meeting ended before he could finish saying his piece, so he followed up with a detailed and closely argued 150-page report on the need to do away with the Chugach, which got plenty of notice.

"What a new railroad needs is tonnage, and you cannot have tonnage without development, but you cannot have development unless you have people," he wrote. "If the construction and operation of railroads by the United States Government is to be a success, inducement must be offered to the settler and investor rather than discouraging them with forest withdrawals."

Graves dispatched a team of experts to rebut Christensen's report. Anticipating Congressional hearings and a political battle, he wrote to a lieutenant, "To my mind this is the most dangerous attack that has been made on the Forest Service for some time."

While that battle continued in Washington, Christensen outflanked the Forest Service in Anchorage. (At least, it is hard to think of who else was responsible for what happened next, although no trace of responsibility was left.) In July 1916, Christensen seemed to comply with Forest Service wishes by disbanding the red light district and campground, declaring that the land would be sold. The prostitutes were suddenly dispossessed and scattered. But the Chamber of Commerce responded on October 2 with a strongly worded resolution: prostitutes were overrunning the town and must be concentrated in one area. Businessmen didn't want prostitution shut down, as the women were excellent customers of their shops.

Without leaving fingerprints, Christensen established a new red light district, deeper within the national forest, along Chester Creek near the alignment of C Street. Prostitutes who had left the territory were called back. Lots were distributed by lottery without cost (and without legal ownership). Substantial buildings went up, a community well drilled, and an electronic signaling system into the town installed. By the time the Forest Service knew what was happening, in November, a permanent red light district had been built on its land.

Alaska district forester Charles Flory laid out the problem to his superiors in a confidential memo. He pointed out that the women couldn't be moved: the port was closed due to ice, and travel over land was considered impossible for women in the Alaska winter, as it required going by dogsled. Besides, ejecting them would cause an open fight and embarrassment. But it would be equally embarrassing to eliminate just the red light district from the forest: the reason would be obvious to all.

"The immediate elimination of this specific nuisance area alone would be decidedly undiplomatic," Flory wrote. "However, the Service could with entire propriety officially announce that it had no more interest in the general withdrawal, without in the least referring to the nuisance, or intimating that it existed."

The recommendation was adopted. When the official presidential order came out, in 1919, it excluded 300,000 acres from Chugach National Forest around Anchorage and on the Kenai Peninsula.

The red light district remained on Chester Creek for decades, becoming a largely African American neighborhood known for music and all-night parties, until it was annexed into the city in the 1950s. Another red light district ran along Fourth Avenue. One of Anchorage's early madams died owning substantial downtown property. The 1973 *Anchorage Daily Times* obituary of Zula Wester, an African American woman originally from Alabama, identified her as one of the city's first businesswomen and called her, "The owner of one of the most popular buildings in town during the early days of the city's existence."

Prostitution was always illegal in Anchorage, but operated publicly until the Internet age, when police closed down the last of a collection of massage parlors in Spenard.

Christensen continued his energetic work. By the end of 1917, Anchorage had telephones and other utilities, a 65-bed hospital, and a three-story school building with day and night classes, 17 teachers and 500 students. His book-sized annual report with three appendices enumerated the town's 1,349 buildings, including the ten barber shops, six grocers, five plumbers and tinsmiths, three soft drink manufacturers, two undertakers, two architects and six dentists, among others.

"The town has been prosperous since its establishment," he wrote. "During 1915, the first year of construction, many people came to Anchorage with little or no means, most of these making enough money to purchase lots, erect business houses and residences, and have, at the same time, laid away money. … There have been practically no cases of poverty, and nearly everyone who had come to the town has made money."

The commission declared that Anchorage was essentially done: nothing but maintenance would be needed henceforth. Andrew Christensen soon moved on to a new job in another branch of the government, promoting agriculture. But, sadly, he seems to have ended life with disappointment in his great accomplishment.

In 1935, Christensen had ended up in Great Neck, New York, where he wrote a letter to *Time* magazine denouncing the dream of Alaska development with as much passion as he had once devoted to boosting it. The magazine had reported on a federal Depression-relief project to send farming colonists to the Matanuska Valley. It promoted their prospects with the kind of exaggeration once used by Christensen and the builders of the railroad. Now Christensen predicted the colony would fail.

Christensen now called Alaska, "the spoiled child of Uncle Sam," producer of unpalatable, watery potatoes, and, "a place of impossible conditions, where there are no resources to justify a permanent population."

And it was true, at least for Anchorage, that no real purpose had yet been found for the investment of building the railroad and the town. The town supported the railroad and the railroad supported the town. Conservation had not been the problem, after all.

# Chapter 4

## Nellie Brown: Small Town Anchorage

*Nellie Brown and Buddy, a retriever. Courtesy of Mary Barry.*

Nellie Brown may have had more fun in Anchorage than anyone else in its history. That she had a lot of fun is demonstrated by many stories and by thousands of photographs, in which she smiles mischievously or broadly, wears costumes, paddles a canoe, raises a glass or poses as a sultry Indian maiden. She was lovely and petite and became painter Sydney Laurence's favorite life model. That she had more fun than most is also a factor of time. She lived in Anchorage before anyone else and stayed until she died here in 1978.

Residents of Anchorage from before World War II had many warm memories of those days. After the departure of railroad construction workers and wealth seekers, well before the railroad was completed in 1923, Anchorage settled down to be a quiet, comfortable little town with an economy as stable and unchanging as a government pension. It lived entirely off the railroad's biweekly payroll, funded by annual Congressional appropriations. There was a single main street, Fourth Avenue, a swimming beach at Lake Spenard, pond skating with bonfires near Ship Creek, a ski jump, dances every Friday night, and parades and festivals for holidays.

"Everyone's father worked on the railroad," recalled Albert Bailey, 70 years later (in the 1990s). "We would walk to school, and these men were—nobody had a car—these men were walking to work. You knew, then, if you goofed off they would tell on you."

"Everybody was so friendly, it was just wonderful," said Lorene Harrison.

Bailey and Harrison were children in Anchorage's early days. Nellie Brown arrived as a newlywed. Born east of Cordova in the Native village of Eyak, before it was obliterated by the Copper River and Northwest Railway, she spent most of her youth at a boarding school for Native children in Oregon. In 1910 her father, William Shepard, a Cordova businessman, asked the school to send her back, noting he, "understood she has a fondness for boys and we would like to have her where we could advise and help select her associates."

Nellie met Jack Brown in Cordova in 1911, married him the next year, and celebrated her honeymoon in May and June 1912 aboard a series of boats on the way to Ship Creek, where they became the first permanent residents, in a canvas tent. Jack was a forest guard and the tent was also a ranger station for Chugach National Forest.

Nellie loved photography and got pictures of everything, especially of herself in charming outfits. She looks crisp and fetching in a sunhat and pinafore, standing outside the tent with her rifle and black retriever, Buddy. When the town exploded into existence around them, three years later, Nellie and Jack joined in with the action. Jack quit the Forest Service and started a boat service, as well as hiring on to help Andrew Christensen survey the townsite lots. Their own lot on L Street cost $85 at auction and became the site of a log house they had built on Ship Creek. In 1917, the couple selected a homestead, on Green Lake, near the Cook Inlet bluff, north of Anchorage. Jack had helped survey the land while working for the Forest Service.

*Although painter Sydney Laurence enjoyed his position as the city's most distinguished cultural figure, he had knocked around the world as an adventurer for years before landing in Anchorage, leaving behind a family in London. Courtesy Anchorage Dispatch News.*

Homesteads ringed Anchorage, in areas now known as Midtown and Joint Base Elmendorf-Richardson. The Forest Service offered homesteads to citizens within Chugach National Forest to encourage development, and later the General Land Office did so after the president eliminated the area from the Chugach. Jack and Nellie called their place Alderwood. They built another log home and kept a large garden and enough livestock for their own needs. Jack and Nellie shared the work. In a photograph Nellie looks as delightful as always, stripping bark off a log with an ax.

By then, Anchorage's boomtown years had passed. Nearby railroad construction had ended and reduced the number of workers in the area. The onset of World War I increased prices and made workers scarce, which slowed railroad work. By the end of 1917, the railroad-building Alaskan Engineering Commission had to argue in its annual report against halting construction altogether until conditions improved. When U.S. war mobilization hit stride in 1918, the Alaska economy ground to a halt. Something like half of the population left Anchorage and the Cook Inlet region. Even the head railroad builder, Frederick Mears, left to fight in Europe.

The Alaska Railroad was far from complete. Work had taken longer and cost more than planned, and public interest had moved on from "the Alaska question." Also, reality had set in. Congress had approved and financed the railroad on predictions that it would create large-scale commerce, supporting gold mining, agriculture, and, most importantly, major coal exports from the Matanuska River coal fields. The line was supposed to be a trunk, connected to branch lines and wagon roads that would develop the country the way the American west was developed. That didn't happen.

The real probabilities came into focus as early as 1916. Joseph P. Cotton went to Alaska to investigate the railroad's progress and prospects for Secretary of the Interior Franklin Lane, who had begun to blame the men running the AEC for the setbacks, despite the difficult challenges they had met. The candid report Cotton sent back must have deflated Lane's hopes. He said the problems weren't in the management, but in the conception of the entire project.

"If I were to be the owner of this railroad after it is built and desired to see it earn money … I should be very much disturbed," Cotton wrote.

Agricultural exports had been a pipe dream. Gold mining was drying up. And a simple calculation of the cost of transportation and the market value of coal on the West

When Anchorage grew up around him, Jack Brown resigned from the Forest Service and built a boat to run a launch service. Jack and Nellie also owned the town's first well, at their lot on L Street. Photograph by Nellie Brown, courtesy of Mary Barry.

*Nellie Brown was Sydney Laurence's favorite model. Although she maintained little connection with her Eyak culture, but enjoyed dressing up in costume for photos like this one. Photograph by Sydney Laurence, courtesy of Mary Barry.*

Coast showed that Alaskan coal couldn't make a profit. Cotton wrote: "As things now stand, we cannot expect capital to be so inexperienced or imprudent as to put any substantial amount of money into the Matanuska field to take coal out to Seattle or San Francisco to meet the competition. … This is not pleasant reading, but I cannot conceive how any coal operator could apply for a Matanuska lease if he honestly intends to mine coal."

The problems became clear even to the AEC's land and industry booster, Andrew Christensen, the ultimate optimist. After working hard to get homesteaders to move out on the land and produce crops, he wrote with discouragement in 1918: "It will be seen that notwithstanding the efforts of the Land and Industrial Department to assist the farmers in getting a market for their products, but a small amount is disposed of. With the present limited market there is not much encouragement for many people to engage in agriculture… We must have a larger population to make a market for the products of the soil."

With the Alaska population shrinking and export markets uneconomical to reach, the railroad's hopes for profitability evaporated before it was finished. Costs mounted and the enormous effort of spanning bridges over Hurricane Gulch and the Tanana River added years to the job. The price of the railroad more than doubled. In 1923, President Warren Harding finally drove the last spike.

In its first year after completion, the railroad brought in $907,000 in revenue against $3.6 million in operating expenses. Including interest on its debts, the government lost a colossal $6.4 million on the railroad that year, almost as much as it cost to fund federal pensions for the entire nation ($7.1 million). Furthermore, the railroad had taken so long to construct it was nearly obsolete by the time it was completed. To save money, the government had used low-quality local timber for bridge timbers and ties. By the time construction ended, bridges were already rotting and a million replacement ties were needed. Rolling stock shipped in after the completion of the Panama Canal had worn out. Every year Congress would have to make large appropriations to keep the railroad alive. The threat of shutting it down became a real and recurring danger for years to come.

The closure of the railroad would have meant the permanent demise of Anchorage. But as long as the railroad operated and Congress kept paying the bills, the town's economic stability was assured. Other Alaska communities rose and fell with the changes in ore or timber prices and the abundance of fish or fur. But Anchorage hummed like an engine on the reliable fuel of the biweekly railroad payroll. Even the Great Depression mostly bypassed Anchorage.

Civic life looked much like any other small town during the quiet 1920s and '30s. In 1920, the AEC withdrew from running Anchorage and forced the community to accept local government. Residents had received services without paying for them and didn't want that to change—a sentiment that would become a pattern in the city's history. After federal officials threatened to close down the fire department, voters barely passed a measure to incorporate the city. The mayor and town council were elected in November and in January the police chief came on the job.

Jack Brown settled down to long-term employment with the railroad. He was a quiet, serious man, self-taught and well read, and he worked most of his career watching gauges at the government power and heating plants. When he came home from work he enjoyed smoking his pipe and reading a book. Jack and Nellie remained married the rest of their lives—more than 60 years—but she did not stay quietly at home. Nellie attended every party, dressed up for every masquerade, joined clubs, took pictures, danced the tango, took wrestling lessons from burly athletes, and, above all, visited. Anchorage was tiny and she knew everyone.

Sydney Laurence was Nellie's intimate friend. Laurence, a painter and photographer, arrived in Anchorage in 1915 after years spent adventuring and prospecting and set up a studio and gallery. Although born in New York, Laurence had studied oil painting in Europe and left behind a wife and children in London to vagabond around the world. He told American friends his wife had died; she told people in London he was dead. Both remarried, although it's not clear they ever divorced.

Alaska gave Laurence the subject that made him as a painter. His images of Mount McKinley became famous. He sold paintings of caches and prospectors in his shop at a time when such things were still commonplace. Later paintings of the kind became clichéd or kitschy, but at his prime Laurence was the city's primary symbol of high culture—well-dressed, distinguished and highly respected. Nellie drove him around town in his own Model T Ford. When he moved to California, he gave her the car. On her extensive, solo vacation travels she included long visits with him and his wife there.

Laurence painted few human figures, but Nellie was a favorite subject. She dressed up for him as a sort of Indian princess, although she had kept little connection with her Eyak roots. She also posed nude, and Laurence's photos of her include some that suggest erotic playfulness. People assumed Nellie and Sydney had an affair, but Nellie's friend, Mary Barry, never found proof of it when she wrote Nellie's biography.

Nellie Brown strips logs on the homestead near Green Lake, which she and Jack called Alderwood. It later became part of Elmendorf Field. Courtesy of Mary Barry.

Unlike most women of the day, Nellie spent evenings socializing in bars, leaving Jack at home. She loved the company of men and was an expert poker and pool player. She joked that she drank beer unless a man was buying, in which case she drank cocktails. But Barry says spending every night at a bar meant something different than it does today. The social life of Anchorage took place in fraternal and service organizations, such as the Elks Club, Moose Lodge, or Pioneers of Alaska. As a Native, Nellie wasn't allowed in their doors, so she had to meet friends in bars.

Racism was engrained and accepted in Alaskan society in the 1920s and '30s. In the city's earliest days, Christensen established rules keeping Dena'ina people out of town, supposedly to prevent them from infecting the white population with diseases. In fact, germs brought by the newcomers killed untold numbers of Dena'ina in those years and shattered their families and communities. The AEC offered health care to Eklutna residents as an after-thought and to deal with crises. A Native boarding school established near the village was located there to keep Natives away from Anchorage.

Some pioneers remember Anchorage with fewer overt signs of prejudice than other towns in Alaska, but that may have been because of a simple lack of minorities. During railroad construction years Eastern European workers were confined to a squalid ghetto and not allowed to associate with English speakers in town. When construction ended they left and the population became almost totally white, except for some prostitutes who were African American.

Even within the seemingly homogenous population, however, there were distinctions. Lower-income families and immigrants lived on the east side of town, rarely mixing with the wealthier residents and those with unaccented English on the west side. The largest ethnic groups among the eastsiders were the Swedes and Finns. They had their own social clubs to join and generally were left out of the Elks and Moose. Children of those families remembered being singled out for their ethnicity.

*Before World War II, Anchorage was a small town, sparsely built up, and only a few blocks wide. Courtesy of Todd Hardesty.*

On the other hand, several of the town's important early leaders were Jewish, including Leopold David, the first mayor. With its stability, Anchorage became a magnet for Alaskans who wanted to stay in the territory when gold mining petered out, especially from the Iditarod district. Merchants came from Iditarod, Flat, Marshall, and other now-defunct gold rush towns, because Anchorage had an economic future and schools for their children. Among the Jews in this group was Jacob Gottstein, a cigar dealer whose family built the city's largest wholesale food business, and Z.J. Loussac, a pharmacist, businessman and three-term mayor who founded the library with his own fortune.

Merchants passed around dollars brought in by the government railroad. Some worked for the railroad and had businesses on the side. Anchorage had found a successful economic formula, and town leaders knew it.

"The federal government is the most stable thing around," newspaper publisher Bob Atwood recalled. "When you're depending on gold mines like Fairbanks was, so often you keep mining and the little vein pinches out and disappears. When we're mining bureaucracy and federal government, we find nothing pinches out, it keeps getting bigger and bigger and bigger! And we figured we had the stablest of all the governments here.

"The railroad was the main payroll and every year a Congressman would appropriate the money to run it another year and so we were secure."

But as years passed the railroad remained a money-loser and had to fight for those appropriations. It served only 5,400 people along its entire length, and even they weren't always loyal customers. Shippers could sometimes save money by bringing goods to Anchorage by boat rather than unloading in Seward and using the railroad. The railroad, which controlled the waterfront, responded by closing the dock. But that was temporary; competition could not be stopped. Planes landing next to Ninth Avenue, the open area now known as the Delaney Park Strip, provided a faster way for passengers to travel, and the beginnings of roads made trucking a practical alternative for moving goods.

Fairbanks grocers found in the early 1930s they could get food cheaper and a day fresher by shipping through Valdez and then trucking over the Richardson Highway rather than shipping to Seward or Anchorage and using the railroad. To counter the competition, the government imposed an expensive toll for the trucks to cross the Tanana River by ferry west of Delta Junction. With the support of outraged Fairbanksans, truckers used a variety of means to avoid the toll, including carrying their goods across the river in a boat flying a piratical skull and crossbones. One group of truckers seized a deputy marshal protecting the ferry and locked him the scale house. A Fairbanks jury refused to indict the truckers for the assault.

In Anchorage, the federal government delayed building a road to Palmer for so long that community members got together in the 1930s to do it themselves, with borrowed equipment, donations and volunteers moving rocks with their hands. They believed the railroad's boss had stalled the project so travelers would have to take the train to Palmer. The volunteer road builders made it as far as the Eagle River and built a steam ferry to get across before government officials relented and took over the job.

The man behind most of these moves was Col. Otto Ohlson, the railroad's superintendent through its most difficult years. Alaskans considered him a dictator, and not only because he used government authority to fight competition. Ohlson ran the railroad like a railroad, cutting costs to the bone to reduce the federal subsidy, and that meant lower wages and less spending in Anchorage. But he may be the one person most to thank for the city's existence: his savings measures kept the railroad in business until it finally broke even on the eve of World War II.

At that point, the Alaska Railroad finally had an authentic purpose. America was preparing for war, building defenses in Alaska. The railroad carried those supplies.

For Anchorage, World War II would bring nearly instant transformation from a friendly, sleepy small town to a wide-open boomtown with explosive growth and floods of new people. Some of the old timers who

Fourth Avenue and E Street, 1939. Anchorage rode out the Great Depression without much change, a quiet backwater that relied on the Alaska Railroad payroll for its economic life. Photograph by Flowers Photo Shop, courtesy of Todd Hardesty

lived here before the war would regret the change. They were wistful about the close-knit community they remembered. But they also took advantage of the new business opportunities.

Nellie Brown opened Nellie's Diner in a decommissioned railcar, one of the old cars from Panama that the Army was rapidly replacing. It was a popular place, and Nellie used the opportunity to form warm friendships with servicemen who came in, some of whom sent touching letters back from their later postings. A colonel wrote from Fort Bragg in 1943, "It makes me a little jealous to realize that what you meant to me, you now mean to others to that much greater extent."

The military bought the homesteads north of town to build bases. Jack and Nellie had already moved to a railroad-built cottage at the western tip of Government Hill, a spot that came to be known at Brown's Point. They sold their Alderwood home and 153 acres to the government for $2,500, less than they believed it was worth. Nellie said they agreed to the price out of patriotism, and because they expected that after the war everything would go back to normal and they could get the place back.

But after the military arrived, Anchorage would never be the same.

*Swans landing at Potter Marsh on a Sunday in October, 2011.*
*Photo by Bill Roth, copyright Alaska Dispatch News.*

# Chapter 5
## Frank Reed: Adjusting to World War

*Frank Reed. Copyright Alaska Dispatch News.*

Frank Reed's phone woke him early on the morning of Sunday, December 7, 1941. His friend, a captain stationed on Elmendorf Field, north of town, told him to come to his ready room immediately and wait there. Japanese warplanes were attacking Pearl Harbor, Hawaii. Reed had contacted the captain the day before to borrow blasting caps for explosives to break up ice that was interfering with the hydroelectric plant at Eklutna Lake, Anchorage's main source of power. Knowing the base would soon be sealed, the captain invited him to come right away, and then had him escorted away by two cars of MPs with the blasting caps.

The city convulsed with fear and frantic preparations for war. Trucks brought all military personnel back to the bases. A blackout was ordered and residents covered their windows with heavy fabric so enemy planes wouldn't be able to find Anchorage. Air raid alerts came several times a day at first, always false alarms. Military aircraft were sent aloft in case the airfield was bombed. The *Anchorage Times* reported rumors that Japanese ships were near the Aleutian Islands and that the Army expected Alaska to be captured.

The fears were not unreasonable. Six months later, Japan did attack Alaska and held two islands in the outer Aleutians Archipelago. Conquering the entire territory would have been practically impossible, but Alaska's thin connections with the outside world were vulnerable. The Japanese navy could have cut Alaska off from supplies, since the territory had no road connection to the outside world and scant naval defenses. Military planners also believed a small Japanese force could seize an Alaskan airfield that would put its bombers within range of major American cities.

Still, the weak defenses at the start of the war were much stronger than they had been 18 months earlier. A military build-up that began in 1940 transformed Alaska, bringing modern communications, roads and airfields, and an explosion of new people. No community changed as much as Anchorage. From a sleepy backwater, the war made Anchorage into Alaska's largest city and center of economic and political power.

It was natural for Frank Reed to be pulled into the local war effort. Twenty-five years into the life of the city, it hadn't grown much and still had only a few buildings with the permanence of concrete walls. But Frank's generation had come of age in the little schools and on the safe streets and had begun stepping forward with hopes the town could achieve more than the stability it received from the railroad's biweekly federal paychecks.

A club of younger men calling itself the Boosters met privately in a back room at the Elks Lodge while less aggressive men from their father's generation ran the town through the Chamber of Commerce. The Boosters had their sites on taking over the Chamber and advancing Anchorage growth more vigorously.

Frank's father, Frank I. Reed, had arrived in Nome for the gold rush in 1900. He did well in business before moving to Anchorage with his family, including young Frank, then a toddler, in 1916. The father succeeded here, too, with a lumber company and the Anchorage Hotel, where the family lived for many years. He served on the first city council, and he funded and led the private attempt to build the road to Palmer when the government wouldn't do it. "My folks … were, I guess you would say, in charge of the community," Frank said.

*Elmendorf Field under construction, July 8, 1940. Congress had appropriated funds to build the air base only two months earlier. Photo by Hewitt's Photo Shop, U.S. Air Force.*

Frank I. Reed (the father) started the Anchorage Light & Power Company, which built the hydroelectric power plant at Eklutna that powered Anchorage for 25 years. The project took nine years to finish. Beginning in 1929, it delivered electricity through the distribution lines built by the Alaskan Engineering Commission, which now belonged to the local government. The plant was small, producing just 2 megawatts, but Anchorage used so little of its output that the company struggled, cutting expenses to a minimum and selling electrical appliances at cost to create demand for power.

In 1935, after returning from college, Frank M. Reed (the son) and his wife, Maxine, moved to Eklutna to run the hydro plant. It was an isolated posting for a sociable man. With quiet charm and humility, Frank would spend his long life making friends with newcomers to Anchorage and welcoming them into his innumerable community activities. A master story-teller, his punch lines always targeted himself, not others. Living in Eklutna meant driving twenty-five miles of treacherous road to get to Anchorage, a route so remote that getting stuck or breaking down could mean walking miles to the nearest help. But Frank and Maxine made the weekly trip in evening clothes to make the most of their dinners with friends.

World events would soon pull the slack out of life in Anchorage. Japan was conquering its neighbors. Aviation technology had punctured America's age-old defensive shield, the oceans on its east and west. With war on the horizon, Congress and the military began seriously discussing Alaska, which was virtually unarmed.

As early as 1916 a government report noted the military advantages of Anchorage, and the rise of aviation put Alaska at the center of the world. General Billy Mitchell, the father of the U.S. Air Force, had built telegraph lines in Alaska as a young man and recognized the territory's importance to military aviation. In 1935 he told Congress, "I believe, in the future, he who holds Alaska will hold the world, and I believe it is the most strategic place in the world."

In April, 1940, General George C. Marshall, the Army chief of staff, said that the military had long appreciated Alaska's need for defenses and was ready to act. Testifying to the Senate Appropriations Committee, Marshall said the Army's studies and fact-finding trips had established that the best terrain, climate and accessibility for an operational airfield in Alaska were found in Anchorage.

*Anchorage Times* publisher Bob Atwood and other local leaders had lobbied hard to bring the construction of a new military base to Anchorage. It's difficult to judge how much difference their influence made in the decision. As Marshall said, Anchorage was an obvious choice. But several sites were on the list for consideration, and it's likely that local enthusiasm highlighted the city's advantages for decision-makers.

In May 1940, Congress appropriated money for an Anchorage base. Construction of Elmendorf Field began less than three weeks later as the Army's Alaska headquarters (the air force was at that time part of the Army).

General Simon Bolivar Buckner oversaw the militarization of Alaska. The son of a confederate Civil War general of the same name, he commanded with a booming voice and a thick southern accent. Aggressive, decisive and impatient, he sometimes went beyond his orders and irritated his superiors in his zeal to build Alaska's defenses, but friends in Alaska considered him an invaluable advocate and visionary.

Within a few years Alaska would have 300 military installations, including many new air fields and shore batteries along the coast, the Alaska Highway and the Glenn Highway, and a military presence—144,000 men at its peak—that dwarfed the civilian population. Indeed, Buckner and the Army as a whole treated Alaska as a vast military complex under their control. Elmendorf, the largest base, was the nerve center.

*Alaska's top military commander during World War II, Gen. Simon Bolivar Buckner, second from left, on Attu during the battle with the Japanese, talking with Col. Culin, Commander of American Forces at Holtz Bay, Maj. Womeldorf and Lt. Col. J. M. Finn (back to camera). Photo taken at Chichakof Harbor, U. S. Army Signal Corps. U.S. Air Force.*

Electricity played an important role in the relationship of the Army to Anchorage. Bill Stolt, mayor during the key years of the military build-up, got involved in politics mostly over concerns about the electrical system. Born in 1900, Stolt had arrived in Anchorage with his family, who were Finns, in 1917. A thoroughly self-made man, he overcame extraordinary challenges to earn a degree in electrical engineering from Washington State University. Stolt owned an electrical contracting firm and appliance store with his wife Lilian. The two were inseparable partners in life and business who lived to old age finishing one another's sentences.

In 1938, Bill Stolt ran for the City Council to boost sales of his appliances. Customers complained that the city refused to extend power lines, even at a profit, and even to homes close to the center of town, west of Cordova Street. The problem, Bill explained later, was that the elder Frank Reed's hotel competed with a hotel owned by Councilman Fred Parsons, who used his influence to restrict line extensions that could improve power sales for Reed's hydro project. After success on the council extending the power lines, Stolt ran for mayor in 1940 to get the city to buy the plant itself from Frank I. Reed.

The elder Reed's health was failing. He had lost an eye in military service and now his good eye was affected by glaucoma, which didn't receive proper treatment in Anchorage's primitive medical facilities. Unsure if his son was ready to take over the company, he put the power plant up for sale. But with no takers, he apparently considered handing the company over to his son.

Young Frank Reed saw the military transform his hometown. When he returned from college in 1935, Train Day was the city's most exciting event of the week. That was when the weekly northbound came into the depot carrying the mail from the steamship in Seward. Residents would meet the train to see who arrived and learn what was happening in the world. After lunch, when a postal worker sorted the mail, they would check their P.O. boxes. The population was 2,200. By 1940, when the military began building, the population had increased to 4,000. In the next 15 months it rose to 9,000. While doubling and redoubling in size, the city had more exciting things happening each week than Train Day.

Business boomed and rents rose. The power plant became a money-maker. The dreams of the Boosters had arrived.

But Pearl Harbor terror eclipsed any cheer about business improvement. Residents were afraid of the Japanese. Elmendorf and Fort

Richardson had been built, but they had few useful planes or armaments. Residents fearing attack organized to protect themselves. Soon after Pearl Harbor, a meeting of citizens convened at the biggest hall in town, a sound stage that had been built on Third Avenue for the filming of a movie.

Flight crew from the 21st Bomber Squadron during the Aleutian Campaign. The squadron flew B-24 bombers against Japanese targets at Kiska and Attu islands, using bases on Adak and Amchitka. U.S. Air Force.

"Everybody that had a gun, and most people had a gun, showed up," Reed recalled. "The Woman's Club provided coffee and help. And they organized the group to patrol certain areas. And I wouldn't have wanted to have been a guy getting out of an airplane in a parachute. There were too many good shots around."

Air raid alerts repeatedly sent 11-year-old Brooke Marston home from school, meeting the civilian guards on dark winter afternoons: "Guys equipped with a 30-ought-6 hunting rifle and a pint of whiskey, on every corner," he recalled. "So you're coming through in the dark and they say, 'Who goes there?' And you'd say, 'Me sir, it's just little me. I'm only a school kid and I'm going home.' It was interesting to say the

least. There was more danger from the armed civilian patrol than there was from the Japanese."

Frank Reed got pulled deeper into the war effort. Things were moving fast and everyone was needed. A friend who was a Coast Guard officer in Seward recruited him to join. He became a Naval Reserve officer in March 1942 and was called to active service in May. On a visit to the Naval Base in Kodiak he was summarily put in charge of Navy interests at the Army headquarters in Anchorage. As Navy liaison, his office was just down the hall from General Buckner's.

"That was it, I was given orders to Anchorage. There was no other Navy. I reported to the Alaska Command. I was the Navy in Anchorage. I was supposed to know something about the Navy, but I didn't know very much about the Navy. I didn't know much about the Army, either."

Most of Reed's duties were low-key, assisting naval personnel coming through the city and working with the Army to trade supplies. He slept at home in his own bed. But manpower became so short that for a time he had overnight duty as the joint intelligence officer, covering the phone and referring urgent issues to the right officers.

Frank's decision to serve affected his future and perhaps the future of Anchorage, as well as his relationship with his father—something that seemed to trouble him seven decades later. As his health failed, the elder Frank Reed was angry that his son had joined the military instead of running the power company and ultimately taking it over. The company hadn't sold yet, but the younger Frank couldn't run it and serve the Navy at the same time. His father pushed ahead with his decision to sell instead of waiting for Frank to be ready, taking away his son's opportunity to own the power company during Anchorage's coming decades of growth.

Bill Stolt still wanted to buy the company for the city, but he had a lot of other things on his mind. In the summer of 1942 war came to Alaska.

In May, 1942, naval intelligence began decoding Japanese transmissions about a planned attack on the Aleutian Islands. The U.S. Navy had lost much of its strength at Pearl Harbor and the Japanese enjoyed a large advantage. They hoped to crush the U.S. in a huge sea battle at the Pacific island of Midway. By also attacking Alaska, Japanese admirals hoped the Americans would split their forces, making victory at Midway easier. In fact, the opposite happened. Thanks to the decoded messages, the Americans concentrated their forces at Midway, while the Japanese weakened their own fleet by sending ships to attack Alaska without much purpose. Midway proved to be a turning point in favor of the United States.

In early June, when the Japanese bombed the new naval base at Dutch Harbor and landed on Attu and Kiska, U.S. forces in Alaska were still far from ready. Troops and planes flooded in for a build-up to retake the islands. Many Alaskans fled the Territory for safety. Japanese Americans, pioneers in Anchorage like their neighbors, were taken away and imprisoned in detention camps. The Native residents of the Aleutians were removed from their homes and placed in crowded, squalid buildings in Southeast Alaska. Without basic necessities or medical help many died.

Anchorage saw some alarming changes. Steve McCutcheon, then in his 30s, recalled, "After the war expansion and for a year or two afterward, it was a little bit, you might say, lawless. As far as the average person in the street was concerned, you wouldn't know about it, but there was a lot of gambling going on. The joints had B girls, and whatever else they did, and there was oftentimes killings; the gangsters would be killing each other and so forth … But as far as the average person on the street or the average family was concerned, it was not a dangerous town."

Buckner made various orders about life in Anchorage, including asking merchants to hold down their prices and censoring newspapers, magazines and letters so they arrived with holes where information had been cut out with scissors. Concerned that white service men would mix with Native women, Buckner put off-limits businesses where Natives were served, which led many owners to post signs excluding Natives for the first time. Buckner excluded Native women from U.S.O. morale centers until Territorial Governor Ernest Gruening interceded.

Buckner also asked the city to shut down its gambling houses and brothels, where soldiers were seen lining up outside. Here city leaders drew the line. Their truce with the prostitutes had lasted a long time. Stolt told Buckner that shutting down vice businesses would just cause them to set up shop somewhere else, most likely outside town, beyond the reach of the police.

*Anchorage's 4th of July Parade, 1940. The military had just arrived and the size of the city was rapidly increasing. Russ Dow Collection, U.S. Air Force*

Buckner wanted women and children out of Anchorage, both because of the threat of invasion and because the town was overwhelmed and needed every bed. Army families had to go. Frank Reed was in the Navy, so his wife could stay (since the couple was from Anchorage, she had nowhere to go anyway). Bill Stolt, asked by the general to set an example for civilians as the mayor, sent Lilian and their children Outside. The journey proved harrowing due to war-cancelled flights, snowstorms and other emergencies, going by way of Fairbanks, Whitehorse and Juneau.

The job of mayor proved to be more than Stolt had bargained for.

"We had problems of all kind," he said. "Boy, I had problems. All kinds of them. I didn't have much time to think about conditions except I was meeting with the military and General Buckner and I would get together and talk about this and talk about that and try to solve the problems between the city and military."

Electricity was a problem. The hydro plant in Eklutna couldn't produce enough power, and shortages during peak hours came daily, with lights dimming. The military ordered lights to be turned off except for critical purposes and built its own plants on base, but Anchorage couldn't keep up with its own needs. Even after Mayor Stolt's plan to buy the power plant was approved by voters in 1943, and after the war ended in 1945, brownouts continued.

A solution came from a bizarre source. In 1946, a tanker, the *Sackett's Harbor,* broke up in a storm off Adak. The bow sank, but the stern kept floating. The ship was one of the cheaply built Liberty Ships that

U.S. shipyards had produced in record time during the war, which were known for sometimes cracking apart. The Navy planned to use the half-ship for target practice until someone realized the power plant installed in the stern could produce electricity from coal—50% more than the Eklutna plant. The city leased and then bought the half-ship, tied it up near Ship Creek, and used it as its main power generation facility for a decade. In 1955, the ship got a new bow and went to work hauling wine from California through the Panama Canal to the East Coast.

*A moose at Elmendorf Field. Courtesy Todd Hardesty*

INSPECTING ELMENDORF FIELD, ALASKAN MOOSE

The frenzy of the war years died down in Anchorage well before the war ended. The U.S. retook Attu and the Japanese fled Kiska in 1943. The military rapidly reduced Alaska forces, decommissioning many installations months after their completion. General Buckner departed along with the others. He died two years later in the battle for Okinawa, the highest-ranking U.S. officer killed by enemy fire in the war.

Stolt quit politics for good after the power plant purchase was done. Unable to obtain appliances and electrical supplies during the war, he and Lilian turned the store into a gift shop. After the war they operated both.

Frank Reed invested the money he inherited from his father in a variety of business ventures, including an electrical contracting outfit. If not for the circumstances that led his father to sell the power plant, Frank believed Anchorage could have developed differently. The city's electric company, now called Municipal Light and Power, kept its operations within the city. Small, private power companies sprouted up to serve areas beyond city limits. They ultimately became parts of Chugach Electric Association, a much bigger utility than the city's operation. Frank thought that if he had owned the electric utility, he would have kept service for all of Anchorage unified within the single company.

Anchorage quieted down, but too many changes had happened for it to return to its sleepy pre-war life. It was Alaska's largest city, on an upward growth trajectory. Some old-time residents resented the changes caused by the war. New people had arrived and a younger group took charge, with a livelier social and civic life, and new opportunities. The Boosters took over the Chamber of Commerce.

"It didn't get bogged down with the old time bosses and people," Frank Reed recalled. "The city council changed, it took a little while for it to change, but it did get along OK."

Reed lived to age 99. His optimism and charm remained until the end, as did his civic involvement. He was honorary co-chair of the Anchorage Centennial Committee as late as 2012. He hoped to live long enough to see the celebration, but declared himself satisfied with his life if he did not. His many contributions to Anchorage gave him a sense of satisfaction.

"I like the town the way it is. I liked it the way it was, and almost every place in between. I've enjoyed the community and the community spirit and the willingness to take active participation in the community by people in order to promote the welfare of the community. I mean—so I know I sound like I'm a kind of a 'Do-gooder,' but I guess basically that's what I am."

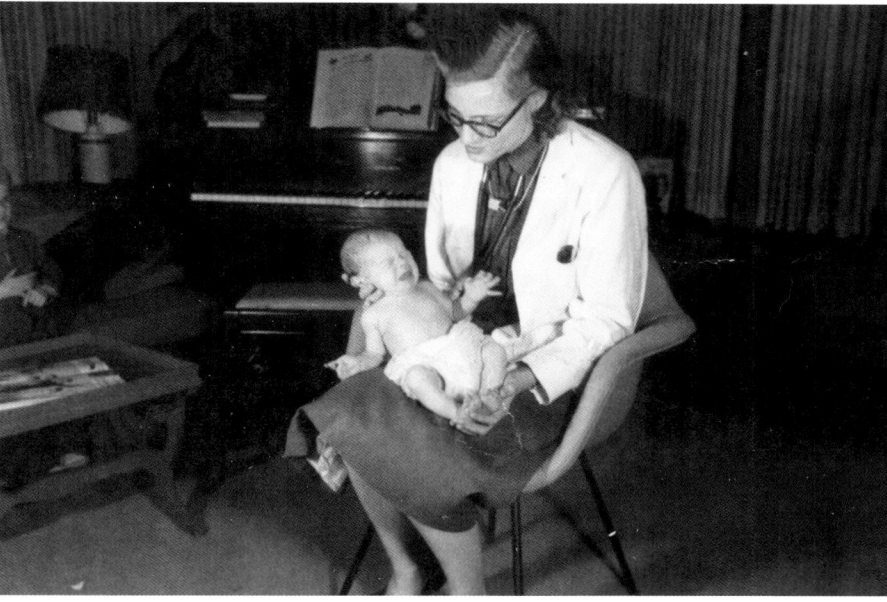

Dr. Helen Whaley. Courtesy of Chris Tower Zafren.

# Chapter 6

## Helen Whaley: The Cold War Boom

A respected physician recruited Dr. Helen Whaley to come to Alaska. Dr. John Tower and a third doctor received the same pitch. All three arrived independently to take a job that desperately needed doing, but that didn't actually exist: providing pediatric care at the new Bureau of Indian Affairs Hospital on Third Avenue. One of the doctors flew out again, but Whaley and Tower, meeting for the first time in 1954 after separately driving to Anchorage, decided to stay and work in private practice, and to work at the Native facility for free. The need was too great to ignore. They were the first pediatricians to enter private practice in Alaska.

The 400-bed hospital had only two doctors and a waiting list of 2,400 active cases of tuberculosis. The entire city of more than 30,000 people had only 28 doctors of all specialties. At the Native hospital, Whaley and Tower found 75 children with no specialist care, many in the last stages of deadly infectious diseases, including complicated tuberculosis, rheumatic heart disease and otogenic meningitis. Children were dying of chicken pox, too, due to dehydration.

Whaley and Tower traded off evenings seeing children who arrived on Bush planes in the afternoon. They took their own x-rays and developed them, performed their own EKGs, and started IVs, because otherwise the children often would be dead by the time a paid doctor came by in the morning. At that time infant mortality nationally was 11 in 1,000. In Alaska, it was almost three times as high. For Alaska Native children, mortality was 101 in 1,000—in other words, more than 10% of Native children died in infancy.

A polio epidemic gripped Anchorage not long after Whaley and Tower arrived, killing 28 people and paralyzing many more. Iron lung machines were flown in from Seattle to keep the victims alive. Whaley worked overnight with patients at Providence Hospital, at Ninth Avenue and L Street, managing the life-and-death guess-work of keeping the breathing machines adjusted without a lab to check blood gases. Soon after the polio crisis abated, an epidemic of fatal staph infections broke out.

Routine care kept the doctors working long days and weekends, too. House calls to very ill patients were common, and Tower recalled mothers of sick children waking him by throwing rocks at his window in the middle of the night.

Whaley had already survived hardships to become a doctor. Her father, once a mayor of Denver, shot himself in bankruptcy when she was 9, and her mother died of breast cancer when she was age 11. Parceled off to a relative's large family, she paid for college and medical school with a small legacy and wages from cleaning the inside of railroad tank cars. She met Bob Whaley in medical school, still only 20, in the San Francisco

Bay Area. Bob recalled, "We visited her uncle who had helped raise the children. He took me aside and asked, 'She's a girl. Do you think she can really be a doctor?' I told him no one could stop her."

In 1953, Bob Whaley was drafted out of his residency in internal medicine (Helen's specialty, too, but she switched to pediatrics so they would not compete). The Air Force sent him to Elmendorf, where he cared for injured and ill airmen. Arms and technology for the Cold War were pumping men and money into Alaska at a rate that transformed Anchorage.

From an overgrown town, Anchorage became a city, with the permanent role as Alaska's center of activity. Schools, housing, utilities and medical facilities all lagged far behind the rush of new people. "People got along without medical care, for the most part," Bob Whaley said.

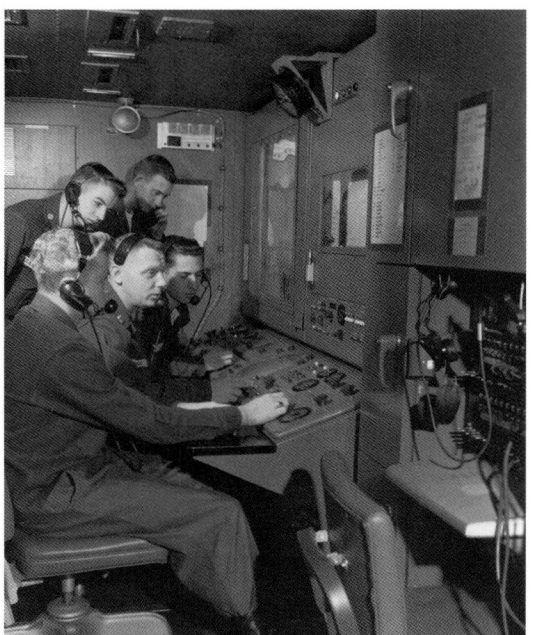

The control room for the first firing of a Nike missile from the Anchorage. Cpt. Erwin F. Tholl Jr., battery commander, is at center. U.S. Air Force.

The new transportation and communication links built during World War II had begun connecting Anchorage to the rest of the nation, but troop numbers had dropped drastically even before the war ended. Then, in 1949, the Soviet Union exploded its first atomic bomb and China fell to a communist revolution. In 1950, North Korea invaded the south. The same year, reconnaissance planes confirmed

A Nike Hercules anti-aircraft missile is readied for launch. U.S. Air Force.

the Soviets building forward deployment bases near Alaska. With memories of war still fresh, some Anchorage residents took to the road and abandoned Alaska out of fear of communist invasion.

Top military officials had already visited Alaska, including General Dwight Eisenhower and the Joint Chiefs of Staff, and recognized Alaska defenses as a critical priority as early as 1947. America's potential enemies were in the northern part of the world and the most feasible way for them to hurt the United States would be by air, using long-range bombers to fly nuclear weapons over the Arctic. Building a defense across the top of America would be difficult and extraordinarily costly, requiring thousands of construction workers and technicians working over a much longer period than the World War II build-up had lasted. Intensive construction continued through the 1950s.

Besides expanding bases and bringing in hundreds of planes and air crews, the Air Force built systems to find and respond to incoming bombers. The Distant Early Warning Line, or DEW Line, crossed the remote perimeter of Alaska and Canada to pick up approaching bombers crossing the Arctic, while the Aircraft Control and Warning System watched western Alaska. The two systems fielded more than 200 sites between them. The White Alice communications system connected

bases, towns and remote systems around Alaska with enormous antennas, and more than 60 sites. That system also carried civilian communications, including long-distance telephone calls. Headquarters for the vast array of sites and technology were in Anchorage.

In 1954 the Soviet Union exploded a hydrogen bomb on Wrangel Island, northwest of Alaska, and in the next year shot down an American reconnaissance plane over the Bering Sea. In 1957, the Soviets tested their first Intercontinental Ballistic Missile, introducing technology capable of delivering nuclear weapons to American cities without bombers. Since air defenses couldn't stop missiles, the Air Force for a time reduced its investment in planes in Alaska.

Nike Site Summit, in the Chugach Mountains, was one of three batteries around Anchorage. The other two were Site Point, at today's Kincaid Park, and Site Bay, at Goose Bay, on the north side of Knik Arm. U.S. Air Force.

*The first Nike missile launch from Site Summit on Mount Gordon Lyon, near Arctic Valley. U.S Air Force.*

Local leaders feared a drawdown that would hurt the economy, but tension with the Soviets didn't let up. New investment came with technology to track missiles and construction of the Ballistic Missile Early Warning System, or BMEWS. In the early 1960s, Soviet tactics also prompted renewed spending on air defense. The Soviets began flying bombers to test Alaska airspace, demanding a response with more and better U.S. planes.

In 1959, the Army installed three Nike Hercules anti-aircraft missile sites to protect Anchorage with nuclear weapons that would bring down a bomber by exploding anywhere near the target. Soldiers guarding the sites had shoot-on-sight orders for any intruder who climbed the second in two lines of fences. One of the missile batteries now serves as an outdoor recreation center at Kincaid Park.

The Cold War arms race incited fear and doomsday preparations for hundreds of millions of people all over the world. Anchorage's front-line location made the dread even more immediate, with regular tests of air raid sirens and duck-and-cover drills. The government tested three nuclear weapons underground on the Aleutian island of Amchitka from 1965 to 1971. Some experts feared the blasts would set off earthquakes. Teachers at Turnagain Elementary School had children hide under their desks as the clock swept past the time appointed for the 1971 explosion.

But Cold War spending drove the biggest changes in Anchorage. By the mid-1950s, the military accounted for 70 percent of the Alaska economy, producing a boom bigger than any gold rush. With money flowing, veterans who had experienced Alaska came back to live. Jobs were easy to get and well paid, but housing almost impossible to find without building your own.

Anchorage's two banks, National Bank of Alaska and First National Bank of Anchorage, were too small to make long-term home loans—they didn't have enough money—so mortgages were for three to five years, said First National's then-president, Dan Cuddy. Typically, a family would take out a five-year loan to buy a lot and build a basement, living in that level until the first five-year loan was repaid, and then getting another loan for the first floor.

Salvaged materials discarded by the military bases cut the cost of building. Residents picked through dumps on the bases and hauled lumber home piece-by-piece. Under the siding of some 1950s houses the plywood sheathing still bears the lettering of old military signs.

Making it in Anchorage required initiative, but the opportunities were extraordinary.

Charles Brewster jumped a boxcar to leave home in Arkansas at age 16, drifted around through the Depression, joined the Marines in 1939 and fought across the Pacific in World War II. After the war he went to Alaska and landed a construction job on Elmendorf, without qualifications. He used his paycheck and his new skills to build a duplex in Mountain View. With officers paying rent in the duplex, he put it up as security for a $3,000 loan from Elmer Rasmuson at NBA to build a laundry. From that start he opened a clothing store that became an Anchorage institution and accumulated real estate holdings, including land in Hawaii and 300 acres on the Anchorage hillside.

Walter Hickel, a sharecropper's son from Kansas born with severe dyslexia that made it extremely difficult for him to read and write throughout his life, became one of Alaska's richest and most powerful men. Hickel made it to Anchorage in 1940 by borrowing money in the street and at first slept on the sidewalk, without warm clothes, taking water from a fire hydrant and catching free meals wherever he could. But he had the qualities the town needed in a period of explosive growth: total confidence, ambition and a quick mind.

In the midst of a housing shortage, Hickel quit his hourly jobs and started building houses with a couple of friends. When he finished his own house in 1947 he used that asset to build three more units near Fireweed Lane and Spenard Road, with help from First National, which had taken the property over in a foreclosure. Betting that asset, he found a partner who owned land to build eight more units. In exchange for the land and an investment, the partner got 50 percent of the project, a formula Hickel used several times. Rentals on those eight units brought in $1,000 a month, while the building had cost only $25,000 to construct. Next came eight units at 12th and G, 40 units on Northern Lights Boulevard, then 96 units at Susitna View Park. All were completed by 1952, by which time Hickel's credit with suppliers and tradesmen was so good he built the town's best hotel without taking out a loan. The lumber yard put the materials on his tab.

Hickel was hospitalized for exhaustion in 1953, but he soon took on even bigger projects. He bet his entire fortune, over and over again, even after he was already a millionaire, to make a much larger fortune.

"I remember my good friends in '53 saying, Wally, stop now, just pay for what you've got, just stop, stop, don't take any more chances," Hickel recalled. "I just walked away."

After that conversation, he built his largest projects and accumulated the vast majority of his wealth. Hickel's strategy worked in the Anchorage of the 1950s, when opportunities rewarded aggressive risk-taking year after year.

The abundance of land and a friendly banker also helped. Warren Cuddy and his son Dan, at First National, financed Hickel's projects as long as they could, then connected him to Seattle bankers who could make larger loans. Dan Cuddy still presides in a corner office at the bank at C Street and 36th Avenue, where, he recalled, a homesteader could have staked a claim in those days. "We used to come out here and trap muskrats," he said.

Hickel considered himself a member of the First National faction in town, along with helicopter pioneer Carl Brady and *Anchorage Daily News* publisher Norman Brown. Hickel saw the opposing National Bank of Alaska clique as a barrier to his freewheeling development career. That group included banker Rasmuson, *Anchorage Times* publisher Bob Atwood, hotel manager Wilbur Wester, and other downtown businessmen.

Cuddy downplays the competition between the two banks, and everyone remained friendly in public, but several businessmen from the period confirmed that they had to choose to be on one side or the other. Wilda Marston arrived at this time as a single woman, later to become a strong community leader. She told a historian she was told to pick sides among two women's social sets. She joined the League of Women Voters, led by Atwood's wife, Evangeline, who was the town's social queen.

The differences weren't only social. Hickel's fast pace and impulsive nature ran into Rasmuson's caution and support for careful community planning and controlled development. When Vic Fischer arrived in 1950 with his then-wife, Gloria, to be Alaska's first town planner for the federal Bureau of Land Management, their second evening meal was a dinner party with Rasmuson and architect Ed Crittenden and their wives, Lile and Kit. Rasmuson wanted Fischer to be the town's planning director. At the meal the Fischers were also recruited into the community theater and various other organizations.

They were instant members of a set of young, exciting friends, the generation that helped start many of Anchorage's cultural institutions. In 1955, the Cook Inlet Historical Society held its first meeting; it would eventually help Rasmuson, as mayor, to create the Anchorage Museum. The same year, the Z.J. Loussac Library opened at Fifth Avenue and F Street, funded by a gift from Loussac, a pharmacist and three-time mayor. In 1957, a committee convinced Alaska Methodist University to locate in Anchorage, which became Alaska Pacific University.

The Anchorage International Airport opened in 1951 and in 1954 Scandinavian Airlines System began landing there to refuel on flights over the North Pole, linking Copenhagen and Los Angeles. Other airlines followed on flights connecting the continents, and Anchorage suddenly went from being a remote outpost to a cosmopolitan city frequently visited by important people and performing artists, passing through.

The slogan "Air-Crossroads of the World" lasted for the rest of the Cold War, dying out only when the Soviet Union collapsed, Russia opened its airspace, and long range aircraft no longer needed to land in Anchorage.

Anchorage International Airport opened in 1951 and began receiving polar flights from Europe in 1954. This image is from 1953. Copyright Alaska Dispatch News.

More important for ordinary Anchorage residents, connections to Seattle became much easier in the 1950s. Northwest Airlines connected the two cities beginning in 1946 and Alaska Airlines joined the route in 1951, buying its first jet in 1961. The company, founded and grown in Alaska, is now the seventh largest airline in North America.

Like the airport, the Native hospital created a new basic industry for Anchorage, in its economic role as a center for services. Territorial Governor Ernest Gruening and *Times* publisher Atwood supported U.S.

Public Health Service leaders lobbying Congress for the hospital in the late 1940s. A report authored by Thomas Parran provided the evidence. Life expectancy for Alaska Natives was 30.5 years and 2.5 percent of the Native population had tuberculosis.

After Congress approved the project, Anchorage and Palmer vied to host the facility. Anchorage won with a site at Third Avenue and Gambell Street near utilities, the railroad, and the city's services. The building opened late in 1953 and became a center of Alaska Native life and the heart of state-wide health care system for the next 44 years, before moving to the U-Med District. It became the core of a major part of the Anchorage economy. Today health and education employ 16 percent of Anchorage workers, the second largest sector in the city.

In the early Cold War, Anchorage couldn't attract enough qualified health care workers and teachers. Doctors could live easier and make more money staying in the Lower 48. Those who came, like Helen Whaley and her husband, Robert, enjoyed the freedom and opportunity for personal achievement offered by practicing medicine on a frontier. Everything they did seemed new. As Gloria Fischer said, if you dug an outhouse you felt like you were helping build Alaska.

The afternoon Anchorage Times was the city's largest newspaper from its founding until the 1980s. The paper closed in 1992. This January, 1957, photo from the paper's archives shows carriers Don Smith, left, and Mike Roach. Copyright Alaska Dispatch News.

Helen's personality was quiet and focused and she thrived on challenges. A brilliant clinician, she never stopped studying. Like all of their young set, the couple enjoyed the outdoors. Robert flew as a doctor and for recreation. Helen would take medical journals along on their flights and sit on the riverbank reading while he fished. After a few years of practicing medicine they spent time in Boston, where she studied brain damage in children. They enjoyed the interlude, but had no doubt they would return to Alaska, where they were making history rather than, as in Boston, being part of huge organizations.

Leaders worked hard recruiting professional people and stable families into Anchorage—people like the Fischers or Whaleys—to build a community out of a town that looked like a construction camp. Single young men working for the summer streamed through the city, frequenting the bars and prostitutes on Fourth Avenue and keeping the Eastchester red light district rocking with music, drinking and sex. A seedy underworld grew up around those areas, full of vice and violent crime. A slang term was invented for shooting your spouse: a "Spenard divorce." The relatively tiny cadre of involved, long-term residents built a safe and friendly town for families within a rip-roaring boomtown, and tried to cope with the growth.

A 1953 parade float for Keith and Clara's Place, a restaurant on today's Old Seward Highway south of Huffman Road. Piggy Wiggly, in the background, was the main grocery store in town. Photo by Bruce Campbell, copyright Alaska Dispatch News.

Fischer's first home, a one-room cabin off Fifteenth Avenue and F Street, had an expansive view to the south without a single building light to break the winter darkness. But development was eating land at a viral pace. The BLM's head Alaska land planner from the era, Harold "Jorgy" Jorgensen preserved many important Alaska public lands before they disappeared into private hands. He had the foresight, for example, to reserve the area that became the U-Med District, which then was just trees, hills and Goose Lake.

When Fischer became the city's first planning director, Rasmuson backed him up as chairman of the planning commission. On one occasion, when Fischer was frustrated that the city council had overruled the commission on zoning cases, Rasmuson called a joint meeting of the bodies. Besides being a banker and one of the town's most powerful men, he was also brilliant, well educated, and capable of speaking with great authority. He lectured the council about the economic advantages of a well-built community.

Fischer said, "Here was a banker who was making a better case, a more rational case, than any planning professor I'd ever heard at MIT or at any planning conference. And it was very impressive." After the session, the council got back in line.

The city annexed outlying areas as rapidly as possible so that new growth could come under planning guidelines and pay taxes for services. Reaching beyond the city, Fischer and the commission drew a plan that designated greenbelts crossing the Anchorage bowl along the creeks. In the 1960s, as mayor, Rasmuson presided over a successful bond issue to buy back residential land along Chester Creek to reassemble the greenbelt there.

But growth spread much faster than Anchorage's city boundaries did, and residents of outlying areas didn't want to pay city taxes or come under city controls. Spenard created a Public Utility District instead of a town government and resisted annexation. The East Chester red light district threw a blowout party the night before annexation became official and city police showed up to keep order.

The Anchorage Independent School District was the only local government for the entire bowl, with local taxing power outside the city, and it struggled with massive overcrowding and underfunding during the Cold War Era. Although the military paid some of the schools' costs, it also brought

Fifth Avenue in early July, 1953. Mount Spurr volcano had just coated the city with powdery ash. Photograph by Bruce Campbell, copyright Anchorage Dispatch News.

unpredictable surges of new students to town. Classes jammed into churches, social halls, community centers, the YMCA, the American Legion and the National Guard drill hall. School buildings, some of them cobbled together from metal Quonset huts, had two shifts of students per day. Money was so short kindergarten was cancelled for more than a decade. But residents outside the city limits repeatedly voted down a tax hike for a new high school, which inside-city voters supported and campaigned for.

"I think the tax was defeated by carpetbaggers who want to grab all the money they can and then go Outside," said School Board President U.S. Hanshew in 1952. Evangeline Atwood led an investigation of the election by the League of Women Voters, finding that questionable ballots had been cast in the opposing areas of Mountain View, Spenard and East Chester. The League recommended that voters be required to present identification and that election clerks be trained and have maps of the districts.

Voters had trouble accepting the idea of the large, modern school envisioned on Romig Hill, to be called Anchorage High School (today

Historians have worked to preserve and reuse the Nike missile sites in Anchorage. The Kincaid Park Outdoor Center Chalet is part of the former Nike Site Point. Jim Renkert, right, director of Friends of Nike Site Summit, is shown at Kincaid with Nike veteran Ron Parshall, of San Francisco, in 2009. Photograph by Bill Roth, copyright Alaska Dispatch News.

it is known as West High School). At a school board meeting audience members demanded to know, "Why was so much land purchased for a high school site?" and "Why did you spend so much money for 'view' property when the school does not have enough funds to continue kindergarten?" and "Why was the site for the high school chosen so far from the city?"

The high school eventually was funded through local bonds and federal grants. When an arson fire burned the only auditorium in town, at the old high school site at Fifth Avenue and G Street, the district added a 2,000-seat auditorium to the plans for the new school. The school became an overwhelming source of community pride when it was completed in 1955, with a modern look and a grand scale far exceeding anything seen before in Alaska. For thirty years the auditorium was the city's main performance space. Ray Charles, the Berlin Philharmonic Orchestra and the Grateful Dead all played there. But Anchorage grew so fast that the school was overcrowded and triple-shifted from the day it opened, with students from junior high to community college.

The schools couldn't find enough qualified teachers for all the new students and resorted to hiring some who lacked a bachelor's degree. Anchorage had no institution for adult education. School board member Jim Parsons recalled asking University of Alaska President Ernest Patty to set up UA summer classes for teachers in Anchorage. He refused, saying the university needed to consolidate in Fairbanks.

"I told him that our Board had indicated that we were going to go Outside to get a college to come up and put on a summer school if UA would not come down," Parsons said. "Dr. Patty allowed as though no state school would ever invade the territory of another state institution. I just smiled because we had already made initial contact with USC, which indeed came up. … The next season the University of Alaska was quite willing to do a summer session for us."

Anchorage Community College, which later became a core part of University of Alaska Anchorage, started that year, using high school classrooms.

The 1950s were Anchorage's greatest period of growth. From a population of 11,254 in 1950 the city grew to 44,397 in 1960. But more important than the numbers, the difference lay in the kind of place the city had become. From an isolated frontier outpost, it transformed into an American city, connected to the world, with the subdivisions, schools, hospitals, library and airport you would find anywhere else in the country. For the rest of Alaska, America had moved 1,400 miles closer, from Seattle to Anchorage.

Helen Whaley continued her determined work in service of the children. After her studies in Boston she brought the first electroencephalography (EEG) machine to Alaska, along with the ability to read the brain wave information it produced. Later, during a fellowship at Stanford University, she further developed her specialty in pediatric neurology. While treating children with John Tower, she also founded the Child Study Center in Anchorage to evaluate physically and developmentally disabled children from all over the state. She started various medical organizations, as well.

Tower's daughter, Chris Tower Zafren, was Whaley's patient as a child and mowed her lawn as a teenager. She remembers her as tough, determined, and dedicated to healing. On one occasion, angry about a rent increase, Whaley hit her office landlord's desk so hard she broke its glass top. As a woman, against the odds, she had to be tough.

"She had an intense, ferocious intellect," Tower Zafren said. "Maybe all those things were possible for her because she was in Alaska, and she didn't have to play all the games that you would have to in a more entrenched, male environment."

Whaley kept working when she contracted breast cancer, even after radiation therapy left her paralyzed from the waist down and Robert had to push her around in a wheel chair. She kept active until a week before she slipped into a coma and died in 1971, despite the hardship of working when extremely ill.

"It was hard for her," Robert said. "It was hard enough for me. But it was very difficult for her."

Helen Whaley's hopes to open a facility for children with severe mental and physical disabilities were realized after her death, in 1973. It still serves Anchorage children with serious emotional and behavioral challenges, and bears her name, The Whaley Center.

# Chapter 7

## Bob Atwood: Doorway to Statehood

Bob Atwood. Courtesy of the Atwood Foundation.

Bob Atwood, who became among the most influential people in the city's history, and a founding father of statehood, expected to stay in Alaska for only five years. It wasn't the sort of place he ever wanted to live. Atwood came from an intellectual family on Chicago's affluent North Shore. He planned his career as a newspaper man with care, the early years to be spent gathering experience at many newspapers on all kinds of stories. He married a banker's daughter, Evangeline Rasmuson, who was a social worker, and they enjoyed an exciting, urban life. With their exceptional energy, brains and charm, the plan had every chance of success.

But back in Anchorage, Evangeline's father, E.A. Rasmuson, had other ideas. He wanted his daughter home and he wanted Anchorage to have a better newspaper to help the town develop. Businessmen had owned the *Anchorage Times* from the city's founding, hiring printers to run it and publishing news that came in over the Army signal corps telegraph as a vehicle to advertise goods. In 1935, town leaders liked Rasmuson's idea to hand the paper over to Atwood on easy terms from his bank.

Anchorage had dirt streets, wood-frame buildings and fewer than 2,500 residents. With five employees and a hand-fed, single-sheet press, the *Anchorage Times* had a circulation of only 650 copies and had never employed a trained journalist. Atwood was covering the courthouse at a newspaper in Worcester, Massachusetts, a job he loved. He was willing to consider a brief deviation from his career plan only as a lark.

"It sounds impossible to run a daily paper in that size of a community, but it was a daily and we decided it would be an adventure," Atwood recalled six decades later. "Let's take a flier and go to Alaska now that we can afford it, waste a few years, perhaps, but have fun."

When Atwood got off the train in Anchorage as newspaper editor, he became an instant town leader. But not of the town he wanted. The arrival of the train itself was the biggest news each week. He was soon bored and felt isolated.

"Isolation was the thing that dominated everything. You were all alone," Atwood recalled. "You could walk to the edge of the city and there was wilderness 500 miles beyond you. Nothing. No roads. No nothing. Very few airports even in that day. Bush flying was just beginning to take shape. There was no long distance telephone service, no airmail, nothing. No roads went anywhere. You couldn't drive from Anchorage to Palmer, even."

Atwood energetically took on fights to build Anchorage into a more interesting town. He identified with the boosters, young men who were better educated and more aggressive than the first settlers. Atwood in particular saw that federal spending would be the source of Anchorage's economic base and its hope for growth. His newspaper became a tool for mobilizing the community to lobby the government.

"I started writing editorials about how bureaucrats were good," Atwood said.

For one thing, bureaucrats would make for better dinner companions. As Atwood often recalled, Anchorage's few restaurants had lunch counters and oil-cloth-covered tables. Formal dinners took place

*After the U.S. Senate voted to admit Alaska to the union, the Anchorage Times published a special June 30, 1958, edition with a banner headline that read, simply, "WE'RE IN". Copyright Alaska Dispatch News.*

at home, but the range of potential guests allowed for little variety. After innumerable evenings with the banking Cuddy and Rasmuson families, everyone got so tired of each other's stories that they resorted to parlor games—one game involved climbing around the back of a chair without touching the floor.

Atwood participated in the campaign to persuade the Army to build its new base in Anchorage, and believed that when it did so, in 1940, his lobbying had made the difference. The military brought officers, men who could fill out the table at a dinner party in dress uniform (he even got the top Army commander, General Buckner, to do the trick of climbing around the back of a chair).

"We can have a dinner party and not have a bunch of railroad conductors and brakemen," he said. "Yes, that's what we had. We lived with it. They're good people but they don't know anything and they're not inspiring."

Atwood said he and other young town leaders would have left without the influx of more engaging people. Instead, he believed his work had changed Anchorage, making it more livable for him, his wife and friends.

The experience gave Atwood a taste for crusading. He devoted himself to growing Anchorage into an urban American city where people like him would like to live, with cultural and recreational amenities and bright society. No line existed between his work and community activities. He used his news columns to push his civic causes. He spoke as a representative of Anchorage to the government, the railroad and outside business interests. He even claimed to have taken over a grand jury to clean up the police department, then corrupted by gambling and prostitution gangs (as Atwood explained it, he was seated on the grand jury by chance and took advantage of its ability to issue subpoenas and indictments without the approval of the prosecutor).

His energy seemed limitless. He was the newspapers' reporter, editor and publisher. He would sometimes slip away from the dinner table to dash off an editorial.

His biggest crusade, and the one that made the greatest difference in connecting Anchorage to America, was the movement to make Alaska a state. Without the rise of Anchorage and Atwood's leadership, it probably would have taken much longer. During the statehood movement, military spending blew up Anchorage into Alaska's dominant city in population, economic power and dynamism. Thanks to Atwood, Anchorage was the first and most important Alaska city to throw itself behind statehood. The story of how Alaska became a state is an Anchorage story.

After the United States bought Russia's rights to Alaska in 1867, it did almost nothing with the purchase for decades. Mining and fish packing companies built large, profitable operations long before a proper government was established. Congress set up the Territorial Legislature in 1912, but it had minimal power and hardly any money.

Alaska's governor was appointed by the President and reported to the Secretary of the Interior. Many purely local matters required an act of Congress or presidential order—for example, Anchorage couldn't borrow money to build a school without Congressional approval. A single, non-voting delegate represented Alaska in the Congress. Alaskans couldn't vote for president or anyone else with real power. The system made for ineffective government and a frustrating sense of powerlessness.

Leaders in Washington, D.C., and Juneau understood these problems and rejected repeated proposals to address them. Fishing and mining companies were getting a great deal and didn't want it to change: the federal government allowed them to take resources without interference and they paid hardly any taxes. Mostly based in Seattle, these business interests had influence in Congress that Alaskans did not.

Salmon canners and mine owners controlled politics even within Alaska. Most people lived in small towns where the companies were dominant employers. In addition, an unbalanced system of legislative elections made it easy to block reforms. Congress divided Alaska election districts based on land area, not population (it followed the lines of the Territory's four judicial districts). In the sparsely populated northern part of the Territory a tiny vote could elect a legislator. Companies opposing taxation or other reforms easily controlled those seats.

The strongest reason for Alaska to become a state was to give residents control over their own government and resources.

A champion appeared in 1939, when President Franklin Roosevelt appointed Ernest Gruening governor of Alaska. Gruening was the president's friend and a well-connected New York intellectual with a medical degree from Harvard that he didn't use. Before coming to Alaska he had already led a successful career as editor for some of the country's most important publications and as the author of books. For the Roosevelt administration he had overseen all U.S. possessions.

For more than a century before World War II, the world's great powers owned colonies, mostly in the southern hemisphere, that they exploited for resources without allowing self-government or development. Much of the world's poverty, warfare and racial conflict today has roots in the colonial system. Gruening, a liberal and idealist, had already made anti-colonialism his cause before he came to Alaska. As the territory's governor he devoted himself to ending its colonial status by making it a state.

But when he arrived, Gruening realized that Alaska's dysfunctional political system gave him little power to accomplish anything, much less advance statehood. His personality and background isolated him, too. Gruening's long-time secretary, Katie Hurley, recalls that his privileged upbringing and education made it difficult for him to connect with blue-collar Alaskans—he came across as cold and superior.

*Fur Rondy Queen Rita Martin pins the 49th star to a flag hanging from the front of the Federal Building on 4th Avenue, with the assistance of Anchorage Fire Department Captain Walter S. Roddick, June 30, 1958. Copyright Alaska Dispatch News.*

She was also aware of under-cover anti-Semitic prejudice against him, although he was not a practicing Jew. Gruening relied partly on Hurley's superior community connections and personal empathy to understand what was going on politically.

For four years, Gruening preached for statehood with little to show for it. Then, in 1943, Bob Atwood asked him to discuss it over dinner at his home in Anchorage. Seeing what the military had accomplished in Alaska during the war had opened Atwood's eyes to grander possibilities. Over Scotch and after-dinner cigars, Gruening found a receptive audience for his eloquence on the subject of statehood.

It was exactly the sort of refined evening Bob and Evangeline enjoyed. Gruening's upper-class background may have divided him from ordinary Alaskans, but it attracted the Atwoods. They sent their children Outside to boarding schools; Gruening had been educated at exclusive schools in New York and Paris. Bob Atwood, now settled at 36 years old, had forgone a life as a widely traveled journalist. At 56, Gruening had seen more of the world and had written for famous publications.

"Evangeline and I were his students during many nights around the fireplace," Atwood later wrote. "Similar sessions would occur in Juneau where my family and I had a standing invitation to stay at the governor's mansion. When the legislature was in session, I would often drop in, appalled by how Outside interests manipulated their puppet legislators. Inevitably, the subject of statehood always came up."

Atwood, and Anchorage, became the catalyst to get the statehood movement off the ground. Atwood considered Gruening his leader, but it was Atwood's newspaper that made the statehood movement a real cause for Alaskans. (A third former newspaper man, Bob

*The Federal Building on Fourth Avenue draped with a 49-star flag shortly after Alaska attained statehood in July, 1958. Copyright Alaska Dispatch News*

Bartlett, who became Alaska's Congressional delegate in 1945, was another other key leader for statehood). The *Anchorage Times* was the first newspaper in Alaska to support statehood. As Anchorage's most visible leader, Atwood's decision to adopt the cause made it the city's cause as well.

Military development helped give Anchorage residents the freedom to push for change, a difference from resource-based communities elsewhere in the territory. In Fairbanks, Cap Lathrop owned the newspaper. As a coal mine owner, he opposed statehood, believing it would lead to higher taxes (the paper became pro-statehood after he died in a mining accident). Hard-rock mining dominated Juneau and the newspaper owner there was personally hostile to Gruening. Weekly papers in the fishing towns of Petersburg, Wrangell, Seward, Cordova and Kodiak all opposed, as did the *Nome Nugget*. Anchorage, a center of government, transportation and trade, didn't have a dominant resource industry to call the tune, and it became the center of the statehood movement.

Anchorage also contributed a critical pool of talent to the statehood movement. The fast-growing city was full of energetic young people who became statehood leaders through the 1940s and '50s.

Democrat Stanley McCutcheon, who had arrived with his family in 1915, pushed a bill through the territorial legislature to hold an advisory vote on statehood. It passed in 1946, making public support clear.

Walter Hickel, the real estate millionaire, helped seize control of the Alaska Republican Party from anti-statehood interests and orient it to Anchorage. Having members of both territorial parties advocating statehood strengthened the cause in the late 1950s.

Gruening and Atwood's idealistic reasons for supporting statehood were only part of the inspiration for these Anchorage allies.

*A parade as part of a Founders' Day Carnival celebrated statehood, July 1958. Alaskans enjoyed pointing out that if the new state split in half, Texas would become the third largest state. Copyright Alaska Dispatch News.*

Hickel and McCutcheon hoped that statehood would make resource development easier and generate wealth. Steve McCutcheon, Stanley's brother, and also a statehood leader, connected the statehood fight to the old conflict with Gifford Pinchot and the Forest Service from decades earlier.

"We would naturally get considerable land from the … statehood bill, and with that, why then we could … call the shots on what we wanted to do," Steve said in the 1990s. "These things were in our minds, at least in my mind, because historically, Pinchot and his group in Pennsylvania and the ecologists shut down the coal mining in Alaska."

Senator Hugh Butler, a Republican from Nebraska, pointed to another reason why Alaskan leaders wanted statehood: they hoped to be elected to Congress and other offices. As the chairman of a key Senate committee, he vowed to use hearings in Alaska in 1953 to listen to, "the little people—not just a few aspiring politicians who want to be senators and representatives."

Butler's comment caught the attention of a group of young professionals in Anchorage who decided, at an after-work party, to organize a grass-roots organization to counter the perception that ordinary Alaskans didn't care. They mobilized street demonstrations, advertisements, signs, hearing testimony, and a greeting committee of hundreds for Butler at the Anchorage railroad depot. During its Alaska visit, the committee heard from 120 people, 110 of them favoring statehood.

The organizing group, first called "Little Men for Statehood," and later "Operation Statehood," worked through the 1950s to build public support for the cause. It began the political careers of several recent arrivals, including Vic Fischer and Barrie White, who together ran Operation Statehood, and who both went on to serve as delegates to the Alaska Constitutional Convention.

But Operation Statehood's faith in public opinion proved naïve. Despite the overwhelming evidence of Alaskans' support, when Butler got back to the Lower 48 he again declared that only would-be politicians wanted statehood. He told the press, "Most of the people agreed they should wait a while." Public opinion came second to party politics. Operation Statehood fought on through a program of having Alaskans soliciting letters to Congress from family 'back home,' in the Lower 48, to their own elected representatives. But even after national public opinion favored Alaska statehood by 80 percent, Congress delayed.

Politicians expected Alaska to send two Democratic senators to Washington, enough to shift the balance of power. Southern Democrats especially saw Alaska as a threat, because they relied on the filibuster to stop legislation for civil rights for African Americans. A two-thirds vote of the Senate could end a filibuster. Under Gruening's leadership, Alaska in 1945 abolished racial segregation (it was focused on Alaska Natives). He later reported that a southern senator said, "The merits of the statehood issue won't play any part in our decision."

When Alaska finally became a state, in 1959, it *did* elect democrats Gruening and Bartlett to the Senate and they *did* both vote for civil rights. But within Alaska, party affiliation ceased to be the major issue in the statehood fight. Alaskans developed a bipartisan consensus and remarkable unity across political lines. This spirit of common cause produced a golden time in the memories of those who lived through it.

Atwood and Gruening's lives and unusual friendship seem to symbolize each step of this political story—the creation of unity, and its later dissolution.

In 1949, Atwood helped Gruening pass legislation that reformed territorial government, including a key tax law opposed by the salmon and mining industries that for the first time made the territorial government capable of paying for modern services. The same year, Gruening bypassed his own party to appoint Atwood chairman of the Statehood Committee, a prestigious role atop a government-funded body in charge of promoting statehood.

*The Fur Rondy sled dog races that start and finish each February on Fourth Avenue look much the same today as they have for decades. On the first day of the 2014 race, James Wheeler, of Clam Gulch, leads Bill Kornmuller, of Willow. Photograph by Bob Hallinen, copyright Alaska Dispatch News.*

Statehood seemed to be growing close in the early 1950s. Democratic President Harry Truman strongly supported admission. But President Dwight Eisenhower, a Republican elected in 1952, opposed statehood after he took office and appointed an anti-statehood governor, Frank Heintzelman, and Interior secretary, Douglas McKay.

With statehood stalled, Alaska convened its constitutional convention in 1955, which adopted the so-called Tennessee Plan, calling for the public to elect unofficial senators and a representative to Congress to push for statehood. Atwood and Gruening both ran; the Democratic slate won, sending Gruening, Bill Egan instead of Bob Atwood, and Ralph Rivers. Although they were ineffective as a team, Washington relationships became the key to the fight.

Gruening worked his extensive D.C. connections, including befriending a new senator from Nebraska, Fred Seaton, who was also a former newspaper man and knew Atwood and *Fairbanks-News Miner* publisher Charles Snedden from newspaper conferences they had attended together. Gruening gave Seaton the statehood pitch and Seaton made his first speech on the Senate floor in favor of Alaska statehood, a speech written by Gruening. It turned out to be Seaton's only Senate speech, as he served just 13 months. But Eisenhower later appointed him to replace McKay at Interior, putting a statehood advocate in the most important position for Alaska.

Meanwhile, Atwood worked on Governor Heintzelman, beating him up in the newspaper. Heintzelman resigned, an unpopular governor, in 1956, and Gruening lobbied Seaton to appoint Atwood in his place. But Alaska Republicans opposed Atwood as too liberal and connected to Gruening, and Seaton instead appointed Mike Stepovich.

More importantly, Seaton picked a former Alaska U.S. Attorney, Ted Stevens, to be his special assistant on statehood. Stevens hired Atwood's daughter, Marilyn, to help him lobby Congressmen (which, he later admitted, was not legal for them to do). Stevens' office at Interior became the Washington nerve center for addressing the technical and political issues blocking the statehood bill. Stevens and Marilyn Atwood created profiles of each member of Congress on cards, noting interests, club memberships, and biographical data, and matching every Congressman with a lobbying Alaskan with something in common.

With administration support, the statehood bill entered the home stretch. The three Democrats of the Tennessee Plan continued to work Congress, but Seaton requested five Alaska Republicans to come, too. Atwood and Hickel, along with Governor Stepovich, became members of the Republican team, working out of Stevens' office.

The intensity of these days and the passion of the Alaskans may be difficult to recapture. Atwood told a story that helps. At a bar after a day of lobbying, a stranger sat at the Alaskans' table and espoused opposition to the statehood bill.

"With scarcely a body movement, Hickel, a former amateur boxer, flicked a left uppercut to the man's lower jaw," Atwood wrote. With the man on the floor, Hickel sat calmly as if nothing had happened. "The rest of us bundled our territorial governor, Stepovich, out of the bar. It wasn't easy to do because Mike didn't want to go and miss whatever was about to happen. But we told him it wouldn't help the statehood cause to have the governor of Alaska involved in a bar room brawl."

The final vote approving Alaska statehood came in the U.S Senate on June 30, 1958. After the applause, Atwood, seated in the press gallery, couldn't respond to reporters' questions. In the decades that followed, he never could tell the story of the vote without choking up. Gruening and the rest of the Democratic team went to the capitol chapel to pray.

Anchorage, which had originally lit the fire of statehood, went wild with a celebration far exceeding that of any other town in Alaska. A beauty queen climbed a fire truck ladder to pin the forty-ninth star on a huge flag hung by the Elks Club across the front of the Federal Building. The day's *Anchorage Times* headline used block type so large it took up the entire top of the front page: "WE'RE IN." On the Delaney Park Strip, 20,000 people surrounded an enormous bonfire, the largest crowd ever assembled in Alaska, while riders pranced their horses around the perimeter. Parties lasted into the morning.

Bob Atwood wasn't there. He went to New York to appear on network television news shows. On July 7, when President Eisenhower signed the Statehood Act, Gruening and Atwood stood behind him.

Statehood marked the climax of Alaska's decade of optimism and unity, and its end. The friendship between Atwood and Gruening likewise died.

Many statehood campaigners felt a let-down, and the new state soon struggled financially. Bob and Evangeline Atwood found that life in Anchorage still wasn't as stimulating as they liked and they traveled the country looking for a new place to live. When they decided to stay in Anchorage, they began importing engaging and important people to visit.

Partly out of his need for a new crusade, Atwood published an editorial three months after Alaska officially became a state calling for the capital to be moved from Juneau to Anchorage or nearby. Over the next two decades he pushed the idea with the energy, persistence and newspaper power he had used in the statehood movement. The repeated votes and court cases created bitter resentment against Anchorage in other parts of the state, lasting a generation.

Gruening, by then a U.S. Senator, led the opposition to Atwood's early capital move efforts. Atwood counter-attacked in the newspaper, saying Gruening was biased because he owned a home in Juneau. Gruening responded with a letter to the editor, but Atwood deleted portions of the letter, including the accusation that Atwood was biased in favor of the capitol move because of his investments in Anchorage. *The Anchorage Daily News* then embarrassed Atwood by running Gruening's letter in whole, with Atwood's deletions highlighted in red. Before the second initiative vote, on the same 1962 ballot as Gruening's

re-election bid, Atwood included a poster in his newspaper that said, "Ernie, Go Home."

Gruening won re-election. As a Senator, he focused on national issues. He is most famous for opposing the Viet Nam War, and was one of only two Senators to vote against the Tonkin Gulf Resolution that allowed U.S. involvement. He lost the Democratic primary for re-election in 1968 and died in 1974.

Atwood's log home in the Turnagain area was destroyed in the 1964 earthquake, a trauma he said he never recovered from. He and Evangeline built a grandiose house on a former golf course off Forest Park Drive; it looked like a set for a movie about a newspaper tycoon. The *Anchorage Times* thrived until the 1980s, but failed to modernize in the era of television news, morning newspapers and well-funded competition. Atwood sold it to oil industry millionaire Bill Allen in 1989. In 1992 the paper closed, its assets sold to the *Anchorage Daily News*, ending a run that had begun in the city's first year. Atwood died in 1997.

Atwood's autobiography, self-published by his daughter Elaine after his death, spends many pages harshly rehashing arguments with old foes. Atwood appears especially sensitive to criticism of the way he used his newspaper for his personal causes.

"Ralph Nader and other special pleaders often painted me as a powerful Anchorage newspaper tycoon who dictated the terms of Alaska's development and would strongly suggest I was getting rich from projects my paper supported," he wrote. "They were correct, but not for the greedy motives they tried to tag on me. I got richer as the people of Anchorage got richer and the town grew and prospered. Ours was the first paper to come out for statehood and I personally worked hard for it. … Did I personally gain from it? Of course I did. Statehood was a big economic victory for all of Alaska."

# Chapter 8
## Locke Jacobs: Oil!

Locke Jacobs. Courtesy of Jack Roderick.

Locke Jacobs, a cigar-smoking working man, walked into a hotel ball room full of women learning to play bridge and asked to join. The Anchorage Woman's Club wouldn't let him in, but he didn't soon give up his smiling arguments and protests at the door. He wasn't a trouble maker. He really wanted to know more about bridge. Jacobs was an enthusiast, always positive and energetic, the kind of guy who loved the nitty-gritty details of complex systems. He didn't get into the Woman's Club, but he used his unique gifts in another way: he solved the puzzle of non-competitive oil leasing at the federal land office in the basement at Cordova Street and Sixth Avenue, and got rich.

Jacobs grew up poor in a family that bounced around the country. His father was a ditch-digger and he began working in a gas station at age 9. But his mother was an infectiously joyous woman and her optimism wore off on him. He also had the asset of curiosity. Although Jacobs never attended college, he loved to read—Jack London's Alaska stories as a boy, and technical books when he got older. Through his reading and by talking with co-workers he picked up a bit of geology along the way.

Jacobs arrived in Alaska in 1947. Plentiful jobs and adventures were drawing young people north. He worked as a steward on a river boat, the *Nenana*, on the Yukon River, a section hand on the railroad near Whittier, a navigation technician in Kodiak, a mining claim staker in Galena, and a ditch digger for a construction company headquartered in Anchorage. When winter came, his boss on that construction job, Kelly Foss, helped him get indoor work, sorting used shoes in the basement of the Army-Navy Surplus Store on Fourth Avenue. That was where he became an oil millionaire.

Significant oil had not been found in Alaska by the mid-1950s. Under the law then in effect, the land office gave oil leases in areas without any discoveries on a first-come, first-served basis, for little cost: a $10 filing fee and an annual rental of 25 cents an acre. Jacobs began studying the system, the geology of Alaska, and how oil companies chose where to drill. In the open community of Anchorage, top lawyers and geologists took the time to answer his questions. He held onto his job sorting surplus military shoes, taking a late shift to open more time to spend in the land office in the morning.

In 1952, Jacobs put his $175 paycheck on a lease, only to find out someone else had already leased the land. His friend, Jack Roderick, tells the story in his history of Alaska oil, *Crude Dreams*. To avoid repeating his mistake, Jacobs began copying down every oil lease application in the land office and plotting them on maps. The project required mind-numbing hours of work that no one else was willing to invest. In the process, Jacobs made friends in the office. The office manager, Virgil Seiser, let him set up an early copying machine to make the work easier, on the condition the staff could use it, too.

Locke Jacobs and Jack Roderick. Photograph courtesy of Jack Roderick

Mapping lease applications as they came in allowed Jacobs to know where leases were available, and to see the pattern of where oil companies were leasing and expected oil to be found. The golden opportunity was to get land near where an oil company wanted to explore. A company protecting its investment in an oil prospect would pay cash for a nearby lease and royalties on any oil it discovered there.

"He wanted to make a fortune speculating with no money," Roderick said. "He realized, 'My God, this is a hell of a deal, where you can get all this federal land that might have oil under it and there's not very much risk.' He didn't have the money to do it, to lease in any sizable way, but his bosses did."

John McManamin, known as Mickey, and Glenn Miller, owners of the Army-Navy, each invested $1,000 on leases with Jacobs, and McManamin told his friends about the opportunity. McManamin hung out at lunch time with a group of men known as the Spit and Argue Club. The usual meeting place was the Elks Club. They were town leaders talking politics, sharing information, and making plans. Regulars included Wilbur Wester, manager and part owner of the Westward Hotel (today part of the Hilton), contractor Foss, city councilman Fred Axford and, most importantly, *Anchorage Times* publisher Bob Atwood.

"The Spit and Argue Club? They knew what the hell was going on," McManamin said.

Anchorage businessmen in the 1950s lined up in two groups, depending on which bank they used (as explained in Chapter 6). The Spit and Argue Club members banked with Atwood's brother-in-law, Elmer Rasmuson, at the National Bank of Alaska. Rasmuson rarely attended the friends' lunch meetings, but got involved with their oil leasing activities. The other group in town banked at First National Bank of Anchorage, the Cuddy family's bank. Those businessmen didn't get in on the ground floor of the leasing opportunity, and that created conflict later.

All were successful young men used to good luck. World War II had imported a crop of men to Alaska who stayed and made money in the Cold War boom. As McManamin told Roderick, "We found Anchorage a

*News rocked the city on July 23, 1957, of a major oil discovery near the Swanson River on the Kenai Peninsula. Oil men flooded into town as a new era in the state's economy dawned. Copyright Alaska Dispatch News.*

paradise and did very well. We were aware that that the military buildup couldn't last and we needed to develop Alaska's resources."

The Spit and Argue members claimed their motivation in entering the oil leasing game was to encourage oil development and advance the Alaska economy. In 1954, when Richfield Oil Corp. filed leases on land the group had already leased, the group offered to give the land for free in exchange for a promise Richfield would drill a well in Alaska within two years (Richfield became Atlantic Richfield, which became Arco, part of which merged in today's ConocoPhillips). Richfield agreed to drill a well, but insisted on paying the Spit and Argue members for their leases. (As unlikely as this may sound, the men willing to talk about it later told essentially the same story.)

The main action focused on the western Kenai Peninsula, on lands originally recommended for conservation by Will Langille in 1904. After being excluded from Chugach National Forest, the land became the Kenai National Moose Range in 1941, and is now known as the Kenai National Wildlife Refuge. The refuge was closed to oil leasing, but the land office would still accept lease applications in case it later opened.

Richfield geologists Bill Bishop and Ray Arnett believed oil was in the refuge, near the Swanson River, the flat moose habitat north of today's Sterling Highway, where lakes and slow-flowing rivers divide the birch forests. In November 1954, Richfield filed for about 50,000 acres in the area, but could not get as much land as it wanted because of a limitation on the leases any one company could file for in Alaska.

Arnett said Richfield asked the Spit and Argue Club members to file on an adjacent 50,000 acres, as he told *Anchorage Daily News* reporter David Postman decades later. "We were asking them to go in there and lease that land," he said.

Locke Jacobs always told the story differently. He said he noticed the land was available without being told, planning to sell the leases to Richfield later.

Whether Richfield told the group to lease or not, a deal would get around the law limiting how much land the company could lease. But it matters how Jacobs knew to file the leases. It was legal to lease the land and transfer it to Richfield if he found the opportunity himself. On the other hand, the company wasn't supposed to recruit outside leasers to get around the law (although Roderick says that was common). This was the same issue that started the Ballinger-Pinchot Affair over Bering River coal 40 years earlier.

The club put together partners in the deal. Mickey McManamin offered to bring in Vic Fischer, as Fischer revealed publicly in his autobiography in 2012. McManamin served on the planning commission at the time and Fischer was the planning director. (Banker Elmer Rasmuson was no longer a commissioner.) Fischer wrote, "I told him I wasn't sure I would want to participate, but in any case I did not have money to pay for oil leases. But Mickey said Elmer was ready to lend me as much as I might want to put in, and that the profits would be quick and certain."

Fischer was uncomfortable with the speculative nature of the deal and turned it down, but a group of partners dividing 14 shares filed the leases in the name of Fred Axford in January 1955, and later that year signed a contract with Richfield that gave it first rights to the land in exchange for a royalty, 5 percent of the value of any oil discovered.

Besides tying up the acreage, the deal gave Richfield powerful political partners to help open the moose range to oil development. The Spit and Argue Club included the top campaigners for statehood, including Atwood. His acquaintance Fred Seaton became Secretary of the Interior in 1956, with responsibility for deciding if the refuge should be drilled for oil and how to handle the leases. Atwood's friend Ernest Gruening, the former territorial governor, helped, too, with his strong Washington contacts, as did Congressional delegate Bob Bartlett.

With the support of a key Congressional committee, Seaton gave approval for Richfield to do limited exploration in a small area. The company made a big oil strike near the Swanson River. The news hit the *Anchorage Times* on July 23, 1957. The town went oil mad.

"It was just wild," said MayJean McManamin. "All these people pouring in, all the land people, the oil people, you know in their cowboy boots and their big hats, and all raced to the land office. It was really exciting."

Her husband Mickey laughed: "We just sat back and had another drink."

Locke Jacobs got busy. He was the only person who knew what land was available for lease. The land office would eventually post maps showing leased land, but only after a delay in processing that made the information outdated as soon as it was available.

When he saw news of the discovery in the newspaper, Jacobs began filing on all promising oil lands in Alaska. He worked around the clock with an assistant and within 48 hours had tied up vast holdings.

Jacobs ran out of lease forms. When he contacted the land office, he learned it had run out as well, but a worker was on the way to a rail yard warehouse to get another 5,000 from storage. Jacobs followed the messenger and found him with the forms in a vehicle with a flat tire. Jacobs offered to help, but when he got the forms in his car he drove to his own office, not the land office. Now he had the only forms in Alaska, and only he could file leases until more arrived.

When he had filed on all the land he and his partners were interested in holding, Jacobs opened for business. A line

*An exploration rig at Prudhoe Bay, September 9, 1969. Copyright Alaska Dispatch News.*

formed outside his office upstairs in the Loussac-Sogn Building at Fifth and D streets. He alone knew where oil lease land remained available. He began letting others look at his maps, for a fee. He hired a staff of clerks and draftsmen to keep the work going as fast as possible. Setting up an accountant across the hall to collect the money, he was able to take in an average of $1,000 an hour as long as he could stay awake (more than $8,000 in 2014 dollars).

The Spit and Argue Club lease applications included some of the most promising land near the discovery well, but they were in the moose range and remained frozen. Secretary Seaton had not given approval for oil development nor dropped the oil leasing ban. When Atwood and his oil partners now lobbied for statehood, they also lobbied for oil development. The two issues also became linked in history, as the discovery of oil created the first clear financial basis for a new state to pay its way.

But Seaton became wary of scandal. Oil development had been closed in all wildlife refuges nationally. The Teapot Dome oil leasing scandal of the 1920s had sent one of his predecessors as Secretary of Interior to jail. Anchorage businessmen who hadn't invested with the Spit and Argue Club—members of the opposing faction in town—were complaining of an unfair inside deal.

Real estate developer Walter Hickel, one of First National's most important customers, and a top Republican leader for statehood, spoke out at the Republican territorial convention calling for competitive leasing in the moose range. Under the federal system, the land office handed out low-cost leases over the counter only where oil had not been found. Oil companies had to bid for leases after a discovery, a system that brought in much more money for the government.

That would mean rejecting the Spit and Argue Club lease applications.

"We were trying to do it in the public interest," Hickel later told reporter Postman.

But that wasn't how the move was perceived by the Spit and Argue Club. "In town there were two, kind of, factions or groups that were kind of associated with the banks," McManamin said. "So,

instead of everybody just Rah, Rah, Rah-ing, they said, 'Ooh, there's something wrong.'"

An influential U.S. Senator, Clinton Anderson, a New Mexico Democrat, questioned why Alaska's statehood leaders were pushing to fulfill non-competitive lease applications filed for 25 cents an acre, when a lease auction might bring in millions to aid a new state. "Are we trying to protect the applicants up there or the people of Alaska?" he said. "Which is it? If we are trying to protect the people of Alaska, we try to get the greatest revenue."

Atwood's newspaper competition, the *Anchorage Daily News*, which banked with First National and had been partly financed by statehood opponent Cap Lathrop, also editorialized for competitive leasing, and supposedly planned to publish an exposé that linked Atwood and Seaton in an oil leasing scandal like Teapot Dome. It's likely no such article ever existed, but the belief that it did created a crisis.

Atwood did lobby Seaton to open drilling. In his autobiography, Atwood would defend work that benefitted his own interests as well as Alaska's. Oil development would advance the economy and the statehood fight, as well as make millions for him personally, and he saw nothing wrong with using his friendship with Seaton, Gruening, and other politicians to advance opening the moose range and statehood at the same time. In fact, no law appears to have been broken.

No newspaper exposé was ever published. Before the issue came to a head, the members of the two warring groups met at the home of contractor Al Swalling. Apparently they agreed to keep the dispute out of the papers; in any event, the issue died. Perhaps the potential damage to the statehood movement influenced them. Seaton opened the moose range to oil development and approved the Spit and Argue Club leases in 1959. The next year, a rig on that land found more oil than the original discovery well.

The 5 percent royalty Richfield paid on the Spit and Argue Club leases continued permanently, through peak production in the 1970s. Over 25 years, the shares split by the partners were each worth more than $3 million. Another group of Anchorage businessmen who had hoped to make their own fortune in the moose range sued over the Spit and Argue Club leases, but lost before the U.S. Supreme Court.

The only people punished for what happened during the oil-leasing frenzy of the 1950s were staff members of the land office, including Virgil Seiser, the office manager who had let Jacobs set up his copy machine. He was demoted and transferred outside Alaska, where he finished his career with distinction.

Tundra swans at Potter Marsh, April 2010. Photograph by Erik Hill, copyright Alaska Dispatch News.

Locke Jacobs continued in the oil leasing business. In short order, he had gone from ditch digger to oil tycoon with a seat on the National Bank of Alaska board of directors. But the wide-open days of individuals grabbing Alaska oil wealth soon ended. Oil continued to shape Anchorage, but the money came through large companies and government agencies, not deals between local businessmen.

The Statehood Act gave the new state the right to select 103 million acres of Alaska lands, about a third of the total controlled by the federal government. Statehood advocates had argued all along that, while Alaska might not be able to afford to be a state by taxing its citizens, it could support a government by developing its resources. When statehood came, taxes did fall short of paying the bills, but competitive oil lease sales repeatedly saved the day. Only oil companies and very wealthy individuals could afford to bid in those sales. Ironically, statehood had made it more difficult for ordinary Alaskans to get rich from resource development.

Statehood also changed the players in Alaska's economy, ending the era when downtown Anchorage businessmen dominated politics. Alaska Natives asserted claims to their land. In response, the federal government froze transfers of its Alaska land until the claims could be resolved. That move tied up development and the new state's selections of its 103 million acres. A stronger national environmental movement helped pass federal laws that would slow down development and force more careful decisions.

The next step in Alaska oil development, the discovery of North America's biggest oil field, at Prudhoe Bay, came about through a complex set of decisions involving many national players. President Nixon and Congressional leaders became intimately involved, and local politicians had little influence on them. That's a Washington, D.C., story, not an Anchorage story.

Locke Jacobs continued to make money in Alaska oil leasing by taking risks and recognizing opportunities. Roderick recounts a late 1960s deal on leases in the North Slope foothills in which Jacobs turned $600 into $1 million within six months.

But by then he had left Alaska. Frustrated by the land freeze, he invested in California natural gas and made a killing on uranium from extinct volcanoes on the line between Nevada and Oregon. He settled down in Idaho, continuing his string of luck with successful race horses. He died in 1992, still full of enthusiasm and fun.

Friends continue to marvel at what Jacobs accomplished. The times made it possible: many fortunes were made in Anchorage in the 1950s. So did his personality: full of energy, fascination with detail, willingness to take risks, and ambition to make it big.

"He was a hard worker, and he just did things," said MayJean McManamin. "He didn't sit around and debate the wisdom of it all, endlessly, he just charged, charged right ahead. ... Yeah, he made his own maps, but anybody could have done it. You could have done it. I could have done it."

# *Chapter 9*

## *Brooke Marston: Living on Shaky Ground*

Brooke Marston. Courtesy of the Marston family.

Brooke Marston was lucky enough as a boy to move to a house on the edge of the wilderness, at the end of Twelfth Avenue in Anchorage, three blocks beyond the city, with a 37mm anti-tank gun in the yard. Amid the excitement of World War II, learning to identify Japanese planes from flash cards, he wandered into the woods, tracing the shore to the west, beyond Fish Creek. On one of his explorations, he met a one-time deserter from the Russian army building a log cabin. Their friendship would form the epicenter of the Turnagain neighborhood.

Two decades later, the largest earthquake ever recorded in North America would liquefy the land under the Russian homesteader's cabin, and 75 other houses that crashed down a collapsing bluff in the city's most affluent subdivision. But when Marston met Lyn Ary in 1941, he was still stripping and notching logs from his 160 acres to build the first cabin. Trees covered the bench, as lovely and peaceful as a forested shore anywhere in Alaska.

Brooke told his father about the place. It's easy to imagine him doing it. Brooke is a charming, positive man, and he would have been eager to share his discovery with a dad who was away most of the time with his war work. Col. Marvin "Muktuk" Marston came out to see what his son was talking about, and he fell in love with the land, too. Whenever his military paycheck allowed, he would buy a piece of it from Ary and from a dentist in Idaho, J. H. McCallie, who had obtained a homestead directly to the east before leaving Alaska in 1929.

Muktuk Marston got his nickname because he liked eating muktuk, the blubber and skin of a whale. He bonded with Native culture and deeply admired the knowledge, resourcefulness and kindness of the people he encountered in the villages. His historic contribution to the war effort was to arm Alaska Native scouts and organize them as the Alaska Territorial Guard. He spent the war traveling the territory by air, boat and dog sled setting up units.

In the mid-1950s, Marston served as a member of the Alaska Constitutional Convention and became an outspoken advocate for Native land rights. By then, the land he had bought from Ary and McCallie had appreciated greatly in value. Newspaper publisher Bob Atwood and banker Elmer Rasmuson bought lots and built houses on the bluff over the water. For the crop of affluent families grown by the Cold War, this flat, waterfront property became the most prestigious place to live.

Marston made a deal with Walter Hickel to build high-end homes. They named the development Turnagain Heights and put up about 30 houses a year. Brooke Marston, now a young adult, sold the homes for

The facade of Penney's department store collapsed during the 1964 quake. The military quickly mobilized to lead recovery efforts across southcentral Alaska, including guarding damaged areas from looting. Photograph by U.S. Army Corps of Engineers, courtesy of Alaska Dispatch News.

Hickel from an office on Northern Lights Boulevard. Lyn Ary had left for Fairbanks, and Brooke and his wife Wilda finished building the cabin, sanded and chinked the logs, and made it a lovely waterfront home with a metal spiral staircase.

The subdivision was completed in 1961. Most of the wealthy and powerful people in Anchorage lived there, including Hickel and the Marstons themselves. The curving streets of ranch houses wouldn't strike anyone as grand today, but suburbia was new in those days. In Anchorage, with its many crude, self-built homes, Turnagain looked like a clean, modern vision of the American dream.

But under the surface, Turnagain was dangerous ground. Earthquakes are common in the region, and in 1954 a damaging quake

*Alaska's U.S. senators, Ernest Gruening, left, and Bob Bartlett, inspect damage from the 1964 earthquake with Edward McDermott, right, director of the office of Emergency Planning, at C Street and Fourth Avenue. Copyright Alaska Dispatch News.*

cracked the foundation of the new Anchorage International Airport. U.S. Geological Survey scientists studied Anchorage's soils and found a thick layer they named Bootlegger Cove Clay underneath the entire west side of the bowl. Tests showed the clay was weak and could collapse when wet or shaken. Evidence of past slides along the city's shoreline bluffs confirmed that it already had.

In a 1959 USGS report, Robert Miller and Ernest Dobrovolny warned that the tops of the Anchorage bluffs were not safe places to build. They included a map with cross-hatched lines showing that the hazard area covered Turnagain's suburban streets. Local government officials made no use of the report in planning development, but it was a big help after the earthquake when geologists were studying the impact.

March 27, 1964, was Good Friday on the western Christian calendar. At 5:36 p.m. the Pacific crustal plate slipped against the coast of Alaska. The magnitude 9.2 quake, lasting more than four minutes, shook, tilted and displaced the entire region. Bootlegger Cove Clay liquefied. Five major slides tore away sections of Anchorage that had been built along the bluffs.

The Native hospital on Third Avenue narrowly escaped falling into the Ship Creek bottom. The slide came perilously close. On Government Hill, the ground under the elementary school fell away in a slide and the building broke in half. Fortunately, school was out at the time.

A slide cut Fourth Avenue down the middle, dropping the north side of the street far below the south side. Businesses fell into a crack called a graben. The slide devastated an area of 36 acres, 1,800 feet long. Along L Street, facing Cook Inlet, 30 city blocks slid toward the water, although many buildings moved with the land and came to rest undamaged.

The biggest area of devastation hit Turnagain, with a slide 8,500 feet long, affecting 130 acres, moving land 500 feet out to the mudflats. Homes tumbled down the bluff and slid out toward the inlet, jumbling into crazy angles, falling into cracks, and jacking up on thrusting chunks of clay. The neighborhood looked like a town of blocks built on a rug that is suddenly kicked into chaotic wrinkles. When the tide came in, water covered some of the homes.

Brooke Marston was driving home on McCollie Avenue when the earthquake struck.

"Coming towards me was a car," he said. "All of a sudden the man driving the car put his arm around the girl and they pulled over to the side. This was 5:30 at night, and I said to myself, 'This is a strange time of night to be romancing.' It was March of course, and it was fairly light. And then I could hear these big spruce trees going,

'Whoosh, whoosh.' They were going back and forth, and you could hear the swish of them. And then I looked over to my left, the south side of McCollie Avenue, and a great crack was in the ground, and it must have been a couple of hundred yards long, and it went through the corner of a house."

Marston drove to Turnagain Parkway and McCollie, turning into his own driveway. It was gone. Instead, huge blocks of earth had tipped up and slid away. He backed up, and as he kept backing the ground he had just been on tipped up and slipped away. When he reached Iliamna Avenue he parked and ran back toward his house, but it now lay below and far beyond a towering new bluff.

"I said to myself, 'Jump, your family is down there.' And then I said to myself, 'That would be pretty stupid, to have a broken leg at the bottom of that thing.'" Instead, he went looking for a rope.

"Normally you would expect, and I was surprised myself, to get a charge of adrenalin out of something like that. And I got none, whatsoever. And I didn't because it was so catastrophic. It was beyond any imagination. Does that make any sense?"

Brooke's wife, Wilda, had been at home with eight children, including her three-year-old son, Erin, three members of the Tikkas family and four children from the Person family. Julia Person, then 8, was the oldest child in Wilda's care, and later described the experience in a book.

The children were on the second floor watching a Rocky and Bullwinkle cartoon; Mr. Peabody was talking when the TV went blank. Moments later, the house began shaking and tilting. Wilda ordered the children to slide down the rail of the spiral staircase to get to the ground floor, something that had always been forbidden. That command, along with other strange adult behavior, scared Julia most.

The L Street slide, here shown between Eighth and Ninth avenues, moved 30 city blocks of land toward Cook Inlet. The rubble shown includes a new apartment building that collapsed before being occupied. The building at top is Providence Hospital, which was also damaged. Copyright Alaska Dispatch News.

Outside the land opened and closed in angry cracks as it slid. A crack ate Wilda's car. Wilda hadn't liked that car, and said, "Good." Then the earth disgorged the car again. Julia remembers her sister falling in a crack and being pulled out before it closed, just in time, losing only a bunny slipper in the earth, which could not be pried loose. At the same time, on Chilligan Drive, on the far side of Turnagain, two boys in the Mead family were swallowed by cracks that day; their bodies were never found.

Wilda managed to get the children to an unbroken block of earth and kept them there. When the shaking stopped the house was at a 45-degree angle amid chaotic shards of earth. Wilda went back inside to retrieve coats and boots for the children and made Wonder Bread peanut butter and jelly sandwiches. They had a picnic on a blanket on their little intact bit of earth. One of the little boys scolded Wilda that she should have known he didn't care for jelly on his sandwich.

Rescuers flying over in a helicopter spotted the group. As Julia Person wrote, "He told of flying over the rubble and destruction of Turnagain, seeing all the land turned and twisted and torn. In the midst of this there was a tiny patch of level ground. On that patch was a blanket, and on that blanket were eight small children."

Coming down from the bluff, Brooke met the group. There were his wife, his son, and several other children holding onto a tilting telephone pole, his St. Bernard, and his house up on its corner, but still in one piece. The adults and children made it to an intact house on McCollie Avenue. Anchorage was dark and cold: all utilities were out of service. Brooke left to get food, water, propane and sleeping bags. When he returned, the house was empty. The police had arrived with flashlights and told everyone to escape a coming tsunami.

Without any way of knowing where his family had gone, Brooke waited at his real estate office on Northern Lights Boulevard. Julia Person remembers a panicked drive across town on jammed streets in the dark to get away from a tsunami that never hit Anchorage. Tsunamis did kill most of the quake's victims, in Valdez, Seward, Chenega and Kodiak, and as far away as Crescent City, California. The earthquake killed four people in Turnagain and nine total in Anchorage; 139 died worldwide.

The four minutes of earthquake created permanent memories for everyone who lived through them. Many said the shaking lasted so long they thought it would never end, or that the world itself was ending. When it stopped, survivors bonded through their shared terror and the difficulties of life in a ruined city. They pulled together and helped one another. Providing safe, warm shelter, feeding people, bringing back light and power, sharing the news—all those accomplishments happened through acts of strength and generosity, large and small, in which neighbors became heroes within their own circles of friends.

Those attitudes, and a flood of money from the federal government, helped Anchorage rebuild. Outside Alaska, the first news broadcasts exaggerated the earthquake's impact. Supposedly, the city had been completely destroyed, or was a "sea of fire." President Lyndon Johnson became personally involved in mobilizing national assistance to deal with the crisis. Through a series of phone calls, he organized emergency action in Congress. A Senate filibuster on civil rights legislation took a one-day break to allow unanimous passage of emergency funding.

The Federal Emergency Management Agency didn't exist in 1964. Until the 1950s, disaster response had been a local affair, with Washington, D.C., helping only as a last resort, when circumstances and politics demanded. Americans did not assume, as we do today, that the federal government would take care of disasters.

But the Great Alaska Earthquake came at a special time of national change. Fear of nuclear attack during the Cold War had set military and civilian authorities thinking about preparation for widespread destruction. As soon as the shaking stopped, the military in Alaska mobilized with astonishing speed and efficiency to rescue, feed, shelter and reconstruct. Also, President Johnson was in the process of growing the federal government, using its power aggressively to solve many local problems. With little delay, the federal government took responsibility for rebuilding southcentral Alaska.

Federal spending created a new economic boom. After statehood, Alaska had struggled economically. But the $600 million spent to rebuild after the earthquake nearly doubled the small Alaska economy, which had totaled $790 million in annual personal income, according to economist Gregg Erickson.

Work happened fast. In Turnagain, Army engineers torched the wrecked houses and a fleet of Caterpillar tractors plowed down everything that remained—foundations, trees, debris. Brooke Marston won an argument that his cockeyed log house still had value. The Corps of Engineers moved it to a lot he owned in Spenard. Volunteers from the Kiwanis Club moved the Marston's furniture and the owner of Smitty's service station retrieved Wilda's unwanted car.

The larger issues of reconstruction were more difficult. Within 48 hours, a team of geologists and engineers led by Dr. Lidia Selkregg, of the Alaska State Housing Authority, began a study to discern the city's future.

On ground that didn't slide, the low wooden structures of Anchorage had mostly held up well. Their flexibility saved them. Some concrete buildings fell apart, but most properly designed buildings were safe. On the east side of town, with firmer soils, damage was not severe.

The team focused on the slides, where the land itself had collapsed, causing massive damage. A preliminary report was completed in two weeks. A national team called Task Force 9 later confirmed and refined the findings. The reports said some of the city's most valuable real estate should be abandoned and used only as parks or open space. Some bluff areas could be stabilized with large-scale excavation, but shouldn't be rebuilt without those changes, and even after stabilization could only support low-rise buildings. Federal officials adopted the recommendations and declared that no federal loans would be made in the designated hazard areas.

The report spooked property owners, who saw their investments slipping away. Some people talked about moving all the intact houses away from the bluff in Turnagain and rebuilding the downtown business district away from the edge. Town leaders were furious. Muktuk Marston said the experts were worse than the earthquake.

Real estate agent and town leader Sewell "Stumpy" Faulkner went on the radio to debate the geologists. "Their recommendation was alarming, that most of Turnagain be immediately evacuated, also the L Street slide area," he wrote in his diary on April 20, 1964. "I said (1) Geology is not an exact science (2) Geologists are by nature conservative and (3) that we need months of study to assess the situation. Something I didn't say was that if we had to evacuate 1,000 families from the slide areas, there would be fantastic sociological, psychological and other problems. A forced move would really press the hysteria button."

Brooke feared panic would mean the death of the city.

"I do remember standing on the porch of my office over there when somebody drove up, maybe a month later, and got out of the car, and he had his family in the car, and the car looked like it was stuffed with things, and he tossed me a set of keys, and I caught them, and he said, 'Here's your house. I'm out of here, down the highway.' Some people had that attitude.

"The question was, will the town remain? Or is it going to be destroyed? Are we all going to move out? Are we all going to drive down the highway? Is this town through?"

The bankers and businessmen who had led Anchorage through its 15 years of rapid growth banded together to bring it back the way they had made it. "My idea was you had to create some hope for the people," said Cliff Groh, a lawyer, statehood leader and Republican activist. "So I created, with the mayor's permission, a reconstruction group, and we appointed a number of prominent citizens to it."

The Reconstruction Commission had only token representation from federal agencies, and a single member of the planning commission. It was a business-oriented group, and it focused on restoring the city, not changing it or improving its safety.

*The U.S. Army Corps of Engineers cleared the wreckage of Fourth Avenue and created a buttress of gravel to protect it from future landslides. Federal investment in the work came with conditions limiting the size of buildings that could be built on the site. Copyright Alaska Dispatch News.*

Professionals who opposed building on unstable ground didn't give up, but lacked political power to win the day. Architects Ed Crittenden and Robert Alexander created a detailed plan for downtown that would concentrate the larger buildings and shopping area around Seventh Avenue instead of Fourth, with lower buildings and parks near the bluffs where the land was riskier. The plan was largely ignored.

Selkregg fought against building on unstable ground for many years, even getting elected to the borough and municipal assemblies, where she frequently spoke out on the issue. She helped create the Geotechnical Advisory Commission—a municipal panel of experts to look at the earthquake safety of buildings. But it was only advisory. Those who wanted to rebuild with fewer restrictions generally won the day.

The shape of the city today reflects the outcome of that debate on each of the five major slides. The site of Government Hill Elementary School became Sunset Park. The site of the Native hospital, designated as too dangerous even for stabilization, continued to hold the hospital for another 30 years, until Senator Ted Stevens obtained money to move it to the U-Med District. The land today is vacant.

Federal funds paid for a massive project to stabilize the bluff where Fourth Avenue collapsed, filling in a buttress of gravel to keep the hill from sliding in a future quake and installing drains to remove water from the soils. Once the work was complete, new rules prevented building on the slope and allowed only low-rise structures at the top.

The Turnagain slide was too big for such a project. Engineers tried various measures to stabilize the land, including blowing up the clay with explosive charges and running a strong electric charge through it with huge generators running around the clock for months. Nothing worked, but in 1966 the Corps of Engineers announced the slope had stabilized itself. The flat ground above would be as solid as it had been before the quake.

But the land on the slope and below it to the water would never be safe, and Lidia Selkregg's housing authority drew a plan for it to be reserved permanently as park. Some of it was, but in 1967 the city council rejected the overall plan, and eventually allowed new streets, utilities and houses where the old neighborhood had been destroyed and plowed down.

Brooke Marston built his lovely New England style home across the street from where his log cabin had stood, which now is Lyn Ary Park. He isn't afraid of a future earthquake.

"Lidia was a good friend of mine and I have lots of respect for her," he said. "And every 500 years she may be right."

It's true that scientists expect quakes of the size of the 1964 disaster to come only twice in a thousand years. A smaller quake nearer to the city could hit as hard, but the Turnagain slide began moving only after the '64 quake had been shaking for two minutes. Earthquakes of that duration are very rare.

The hazardous ground on the west side of downtown Anchorage is a bigger problem. The technical committees said it should be rebuilt only with stabilization, and then only with small structures.

But soon after the earthquake, Hickel announced he would build the Hotel Captain Cook in the red zone, within 60 feet of the graben, where the L Street slide had separated. Hickel used private financing, so he didn't depend on the federal loans. Pro-development leaders hailed his decision, and Dan Cuddy's announcement that he would build his First National Bank building at Fifth Avenue and G Street.

These were important votes of confidence in Anchorage in 1964. The bank stood just outside the high-hazard area and the Captain Cook just within it. But the hotel was built to high seismic standards and with extensive soil studies, and only a very large earthquake could bring a slide to its foundations.

But the city went much farther in ignoring the experts' warnings. Within a year of the quake, the city council rezoned the L Street slide area for bigger apartment buildings and more offices. In its 1976 comprehensive plan, the council deleted all mention of the hazard. No special construction or height requirements applied to the area.

Big buildings went up at the edge, including the Peterson Towers at 510 L Street and the Resolution Tower, later renamed the Brady Building, at 1031 W. Fourth Avenue. When Carl Brady developed that building in 1981, he said, "Buildings built properly can withstand an earthquake, and if Resolution Tower ever does go into the inlet, it'll be in one piece."

Lidia's daughter, Dr. Sheila Selkregg, kept up her mother's fight; she too got elected to the Assembly. Her doctoral dissertation discussed the decision to build the Nesbett Courthouse near the bluff at Third Avenue, well within the hazard zone and on particularly bad ground. Three studies, two commissions and a liability expert all said not to build there, but a fourth report approved the plan. The building was completed in 1996 after 14 years of study and construction.

*Seismic investigations became an important part of construction after the 1964 earthquake. Work is done here in 1982 as the Arco office building is constructed in the background. Copyright Alaska Dispatch News.*

John Aho, a structural engineer who has served on the Geotechnical Advisory Commission since 1976, said the design of the courthouse was improved after expert review. It is built to withstand four feet of movement in the earth. But that doesn't mean it or the other buildings on hazardous ground will be safe in a large earthquake.

Aho said engineers know how to design buildings to withstand shaking. But a structural engineer has to assume that the foundation soils will remain under the building. Having the courthouse stay in one piece is not enough.

"They can say it will hold together, but the orientation of that building after it slides, they cannot predict," Aho said. "It could be on its side, it could be upside down. It's foolish to say it can just slide down the hill.

"It makes zero sense to me to build buildings, major, major structures, along that bluff area. But it's done. And now we'll see what happens."

For most people, earthquakes are not an everyday thought, even though, living in one of the most seismically active areas on earth, Anchorage residents often feel small ones. Experts don't like to talk about which buildings may not be safe, for legal reasons. And Brooke Marston said that those who declared they would never go inside a building near one of the slides slowly discarded those resolutions.

"There are some people who swore they would never come to Turnagain," he said, in the sitting room of his house across from Lyn Ary Park. "They're still here, but it has faded into the background of their lives."

Ary's cabin still stands, where Brooke moved it, at 3007 32nd Avenue. You can see how Ary fit the logs together at the corners with dovetail joints, like good cabinetry. That's what held the cabin together when it tipped over in the earthquake, and saved Wilda Marston and eight children.

Jim LaBelle with U.S. Senator Mike Gravel. Courtesy Jim LaBelle.

# Chapter 10

## Jim LaBelle: Native Power Rising

Hearing Jim LaBelle repeat the nightmare tale of his childhood in an Alaska Native boarding school is like watching him open a vein: it's as serious, purposeful and at least as painful. But he does so every year, calmly and deliberately, for students in his University of Alaska Anchorage class on this history of Alaska Native land claims. He thinks they need to know about the powerlessness that came before the triumph of Native groups in Alaska.

LaBelle also teaches a class in the business management of Alaska Native Corporations. Today, they include eight of the ten largest Alaska-owned businesses, mostly headquartered in Anchorage. Their myriad enterprises involve almost every industry in Alaska and reach all over the world. In addition, Native non-profit corporations and tribal organizations operate some of the largest institutions in the city, including a huge health campus in the U-Med District. The rise of Native power is an Anchorage story. Much of the action happened here, and it helped shape the city's profile.

It wasn't so in 1955, when LaBelle was eight years old. As his life shows, the Alaska Native movement turned upside-down a world in which the first people were barely treated like people at all. Or, to put it better, turned it right-side-up.

The Alaska Constitutional Convention was about to meet on the University of Alaska Fairbanks campus with only a single Native member when LaBelle and his six-year-old brother, Kermit, were put on a plane from Fairbanks to the Wrangell Institute boarding school, 800 miles away in the Southeast Alaska community of Wrangell. Their father was dead and their mother a dysfunctional alcoholic. Many other students were taken to boarding schools from intact Native families against their parents' will, leaving behind villages devoid of children's voices. On arrival in Wrangell the children were tied together like a chain gang, stripped, and their heads shaven. In LaBelle's memory, the school sounds like a prison camp.

"It was a total institution," he said. "You could not escape. There wasn't any place in the rooms, in your dorm, in the mess hall, on the campus, where you could kind of be yourself and speak your own language. There was always someone watching or waiting or listening."

LaBelle knew English as well as Iñupiaq and tried to speak English to avoid beatings, shaming, being locked in dark closets. Children who couldn't speak English were punished without comprehension or the ability to comply. LaBelle witnessed and experienced brutal, unforgettable violence by staff. He was sexually abused from his first year in the school, like many other students.

"At night when the lights went out were really terrible times. I remember, all it took was for one child to start sniffling and in low tones start calling for his mother, and then it would catch on. Other children were left alone with their thoughts and missing home and parents, and

The Trans-Alaska Pipeline under construction at Livengood, June 1976. Photograph by P. Steuke, Land Use Commission, courtesy Alaska Dispatch News.

then they started crying as well, and it grew, in intensity, cacophony, and pretty soon the entire wing of our dorm would be just wailing away into the night. We were all crying for someone, some loved-one in our lives. And we would just about cry ourselves to sleep. And in the morning, we could barely open our eyes, which were all swollen from all those tears."

The statehood advocates at the constitutional convention regarded the Bureau of Indian Affairs school system as an improvement over the complete lack of formal education that existed in many villages before. No one was there to tell them differently. Natives had little voice in the political system. But it's not entirely accurate to say they were excluded. The constitutional doings in Fairbanks appeared irrelevant to subsistence lifeways, with debate conducted in outsiders' language about laws from an alien culture.

But statehood in 1959 and the educational assimilation of a new generation to the outside culture planted the seeds for the demise of the system of white dominance. The Statehood Act approved by Congress gave Alaska state government first choice of 103 million acres of land for its own. The state was essentially a white institution. It had no intention of giving the land it received to the Natives.

Native leaders had worked for decades to defend their rights to lands they had used for thousands of years. The threat of the state getting permanent ownership motivated them to become more assertive. Native associations formed around Alaska and filed claims with the federal government, eventually clouding ownership of all of Alaska. The Democratic administration in Washington, D.C., enlightened by the minority rights movements of the 1960s, backed the claims by freezing all federal land transfers in Alaska.

The white establishment in Anchorage was furious. Accustomed to a system in which businessmen could become rich just by filing for oil leases at the BLM office at Sixth Avenue and Cordova, they now saw the Native claims as a barrier to the wealth promised by statehood. If Natives actually received large blocks of land, many assumed they would use it for traditional hunting and gathering.

"Everybody was against the Natives getting the land," said oil attorney and businessman Jack Roderick. "Even Gruening and those guys. 'Hey, you guys are screwing things up. Get out of here.' … Bob Atwood was against the Natives, everybody was against the Natives."

But a few white leaders saw the Natives as a wedge against the conservationists who had been foes since before Anchorage was founded. Ted Stevens had returned to Anchorage after the 1960 election of President John Kennedy ended his job at the Interior Department. He practiced oil industry law with Roderick. Stevens won a seat in the State House in 1964 and again in '66. He thought the Natives would use their land for more than

*The Alaska Native Claims Settlement Act forced young Native leaders to make complex decisions about which lands to select. Arctic Slope Regional Corporation officials and advisors prepare to make final choices on approximately 4.7 million acres. From left, David Hickok, Elijah Rock, Jacobs Adams, signing, and James Wickwire. Copyright Alaska Dispatch News.*

hunting. Many Native leaders saw resource development as a way of addressing village poverty. Stevens envisioned their corporations logging, mining and drilling land more aggressively than federal managers would ever allow.

Oil and Native power became entwined soon after statehood. In 1961, the state sold oil leases on the edge of reservation land owned by the village of Tyonek, on the west side of Cook Inlet. Oil under the reservation could be drained by wells on the edge. To protect its share, the village held its own lease sale in 1964, which brought in $13 million. Tyonek invested some of that money in Anchorage real estate projects, including the Kaloa Building, named after its chief, Albert Kaloa, but its most important investment was in the Native movement as a whole. In 1966, Tyonek leaders paid for the founding meeting of the Alaska Federation of Natives, which took place above a fur shop near Fourth Avenue and D Street. Rights advocates from across the state sought unity for the first time.

Native leaders met and often established offices in Anchorage as they addressed the challenging tasks of creating corporations in consultation with lawyers and other advisors. Shown here in 1973, Hank Eaton, Sam Kito, Pat Panamaroff, and Joe Josephson. Copyright Alaska Dispatch News.

That same year, 1966, Native votes helped put Walter Hickel in the governor's office. He formed a commission that called for a 40-million-acre land settlement with Alaska's Natives. He also negotiated with Iñupiat leaders on the North Slope to lift their land claim objections to allow oil exploration, which could benefit everyone. But Hickel was hardly the advocate the Natives wanted. He fought the land freeze. Appointed by President Richard Nixon to be Secretary of the Interior after the 1968 election, he declared he could end the freeze, but was forced to agree to keep it in order to win confirmation by Congress.

By then, big oil had arrived in Alaska. The Prudhoe Bay oil discovery came in on the state's North Slope lands in 1968, with enough oil to change the state forever.

The incredible size of Alaska's riches from Prudhoe Bay came into focus on September 10, 1969, in the Sydney Laurence Auditorium at Sixth Avenue and F Street. The state held an oil lease sale for new acreage on the edge of the discovery that brought in $900 million, almost nine times the state's total budget in the previous fiscal year. And, in addition, an oil pipeline across Alaska, the largest private construction project in American history, would be needed to get the oil to the ice-free port of Valdez.

The dream of contracts for pipeline construction lured Alaskan businesses to borrow heavily for new facilities. The oil companies predicted a quick project. Instead, the pipeline was delayed, the economy slowed, and local investors couldn't make loan payments. The reasons for delay were many, including industry errors, opposition by the environmental movement, and the land ownership claims of Alaska Natives.

A year after the big lease sale, Ed Patton, head of the companies' pipeline group, the Alyeska Pipeline Service Co., told the Anchorage Chamber of Commerce the project could not be built without a bill in

Congress approving Native land claims. After hearing that news, Mayor George Sullivan hosted emergency weekend meetings of business and community leaders to organize support for the Native claims bill in Congress. Working from the statehood movement's playbook from 15 years earlier, they recruited Alaskans to have their families outside the state flood Congressmen with telegrams of support from their home districts for a Native claims bill.

But the center of power had moved. According to historian Don Mitchell, those messages, coming from people uninformed on the complex issue, irritated Congressmen and probably didn't help at all. The oil industry itself had more impact. President Richard Nixon had come to power with strong support from oil. Patton told his lobbyist, Bill Foster, "We want a bill passed. And we want the Natives happy." The Nixon administration helped push the bill through a year later, with the president unexpectedly declaring he would sign no bill that that Alaska Native leaders did not approve.

In 1971, Jim LaBelle was a student at Alaska Methodist University (later to be Alaska Pacific University) when Native leaders met to approve the bill Congress had passed. He stood at the back of the room in the Atwood Center with other students—including several who are well known Native leaders today—as Nixon's voice came from a metal speaker.

"All these Native leaders were in the room. It was just an awesome thing. They represented every region, every village practically. And here we were witnessing history as students," LaBelle said. "And we heard Nixon say, 'I am about to sign the Alaska Native Claims Settlement Act,' and everyone went nuts in the room. And he signed it.

"Everything was really palpable. There was so much excitement and elation and laughing and cheering, and I think some people were crying,"

The Trans-Alaska Pipeline, 1986. Copyright Alaska Dispatch News.

LaBelle recalled. "I saw the look of relief on some faces. They had been fighting in earnest for a claims act since '66, and five years later here it is, and I even heard one Native leader say to another, 'Now what do we do?'"

Native people, through corporations, would now own 44 million acres of land and almost $1 billion in compensation. But the hardest part was only starting. The concept of the settlement had seemed logical, to set up twelve regional corporations and more than 200 village corporations to own the land and receive the money, with all living Alaska Natives as shareholders. This set-up would avoid creating reservations, which many perceived a failure in the Lower 48, and would give the Natives an incentive to use their land productively, for profit.

But the new law, ANCSA, had been rushed through to speed approval of the pipeline, and it contained many provisions that proved unworkable or poorly thought-out. Among them, the idea of hundreds of new corporations in places where business opportunities were scant or non-existent, to be run by people with no business tradition, and whose culture emphasized equality, cooperation and collective ownership of resources rather than corporate hierarchy and competition.

Jim LaBelle graduated from college in 1973 with a degree in history and hopes of being a high school teacher. Elders asked him instead to help set up corporations in his wife's Chugach region, around Prince William Sound and southwest of Kachemak Bay. He knew nothing about corporations. He had spent most of his time since high school serving in the Navy. (His brother Kermit had been killed in Viet Nam.) When Nixon signed ANCSA and he stood in the back of the room, Jim was becoming aware of the entire Native claims issue for the first time.

The ASRC building in Anchorage under construction in 2002. The last decade has seen a series of Native corporation towers built. Photograph by Bill Roth, copyright Alaska Dispatch News.

"I had no business experience, no business training. None of us did at Chugach, for that matter. We were all either blue collar employees, or cannery workers, or subsistence hunters or fishers or gatherers, and we were put in this awesome place where we had to become responsible now for almost one million acres of land and this money and trying to figure out a way to make it work. We made a lot of mistakes because of that lack of knowledge.

"We were given this big box of parts to something very complicated and expected to make it work, and we went through a lot of trial and error and failures before we started to understand the essential things we had to do."

The time and expense of setting up corporations and selecting land depleted the seed money from Congress, especially for village corporations. Lawyers and accountants got much of it. The flaws in the legislation led to a decade-long battle with the government over recognition of villages, borders between regions, and, in the Chugach region, how much land the Natives could take from within the National Forest. Chugach didn't receive its land until a settlement in 1982.

Chugach land selections focused on elders' knowledge of important areas for traditional uses, but also considered values for timber, coal mining and tourism development. Chugach village corporations were allowed to pick land from within Chugach National Forest. The same Bering River coal lands that created a national scandal during the Taft administration—and indirectly contributed to Anchorage's birth—now became Chugach Alaska regional corporation lands.

The regional corporation for Anchorage and the Dena'ina homeland, Cook Inlet Region Inc., faced a different set of challenges. CIRI shareholders lived in a region that had already been developed, with lands claimed by the state, the military or settled by private owners. For CIRI land selections, the government offered useless left-overs, such as glaciers and mountaintops.

The corporation pursued a five-year legal and political battle for access to other state and federal lands, including outside the region and outside the state, in exchange for its poor allocations in southcentral Alaska. A three-way exchange agreement in 1976 between CIRI, the state and the federal governments set up the exchange process. The delay also may have helped CIRI. It gave managers time to learn how to run the company and what kind of land could yield the most profit.

"We ended up doing fine in this process because we had taken the time to gain a better understanding of land status than anyone else involved," said Margie Brown, who later became CIRI's president and CEO. Competing state agencies and the legislature overlooked properties CIRI's real estate experts zeroed in on—for example, oil and gas land producing revenue on the Kenai Peninsula. After getting those lands, CIRI also went back to court to get royalty payments dramatically increased.

In exchange for some lands it didn't receive, CIRI received a financial account it could use to obtain federal land outside Alaska. When the military released land, CIRI used the credit and its selection priority to grab once-in-a-lifetime opportunities. A national crisis of failing savings and loan institutions in the 1980s put a flood of private properties into federal ownership, catching CIRI's attention.

"We went, 'Holy cow, our account should be good for these properties, too,'" said Ken Klett, a former vice president. "That's how CIRI ended up with $250 million in properties across the country."

The money it made from lands thanks to the 1976 agreement allowed CIRI to invest in other lines of business. After cashing out stock in a mobile phone company in 2000, it paid $65,000 each to shareholders with a typical 100 shares. A few other regional corporations were also successful from the start. But the twelve Native regional corporations as a whole lost money on business operations almost every year, losses that after the first two decades totaled more than three quarters of their original $962.5 million settlement.

One critical ally saved Chugach Alaska and other regional corporations: Senator Ted Stevens.

Stevens had long wanted to be a U.S. Senator. Living in Anchorage in 1962, he ran against Senator Ernest Gruening and lost. Six years later, he ran again and lost in the primary. But after Senator Bob Bartlett died in December, 1968, Governor Hickel appointed Stevens to replace him.

*Part of a massive march of Alaska Natives in 2002. Photograph by Bill Roth, copyright Alaska Dispatch News.*

Stevens served 40 years, longer than any other Republican in Senate history. After helping craft the Native claims settlement, he devoted much of his career to protecting Alaska Native rights and nursing their corporations to profitability.

Stevens engineered a Native corporation bailout using amendments so technical they initially attracted little notice. A 1986 tax law amendment allowed Alaska Native corporations to sell net operating losses, called NOLs, to profit-making corporations that would use them to reduce their taxes, something no one else could do. In the late 1980s Stevens also made amendments to laws designed to help small minority-owned businesses, giving Alaska Native corporations huge advantages to win contracts for services to the military and federal government. Those complex Small Business Administration laws got the nickname 8(a), for their section in the statutes.

Chugach Alaska filed for bankruptcy in 1991 due to a failed investment in a timber mill, a drop in fish and timber prices, and other problems, but Stevens' laws brought it back. The corporation had sold the Bering River coal field to a Korean company, booking a huge loss compared to the supposed original value of the coal. After selling its NOLs to companies like Quaker Oats and Pillsbury, Chugach had enough money to get out of bankruptcy. Later, it began providing services to the military and other federal agencies under 8(a) contracts, and was spectacularly successful. Ten years after leaving bankruptcy, Chugach had grown to be the second largest Alaska-owned company, according to the annual listing in *Alaska Business Monthly* called "The Top 49ers."

But with Native business success, the 1990s also became a difficult time of conflict between urban and rural Alaska, a problem called the urban-rural divide.

Natives had won the right to have schools in their own communities rather than going to boarding school, but some urban legislators thought the rural schools were getting too much money and pushed for a funding formula that would benefit the cities. Voters passed a law making English the official language of Alaska, even though Native languages had preceded it by thousands of years. A federal conservation law gave rural users priority for hunting and fishing on federal land; that law overrode Alaska's Constitution, which required every Alaskan to be treated equally. Because of that, the state lost authority over fish and game on federal land, which had been a major purpose of the statehood movement.

There were uglier issues, too, including a 2001 incident in which teenagers filmed themselves shooting homeless Natives with frozen paintballs in downtown Anchorage. The paintball incident only involved a few people on a particular night, but it became a symbol of disrespect felt by Alaska Natives. And in the new Alaska, Native leaders would no longer accept that perceived prejudice.

"When debates go on in the legislature, so often it comes down to 'Is this a Native thing?'" said Roy Huhndorf, former CEO of CIRI, in 1998. "I think it's mean-spirited, oppressive, short-sighted and outright racist in some cases."

Natives mounted a huge march through downtown Anchorage to protest their perception of the state's racial prejudice. The march angered some powerful white leaders, including Ramona Barnes, who represented East Anchorage in the State House from 1978 to 1984 and from 1986 to 2000. She told a reporter, "Most people in urban areas feel they have been discriminated against because of all the money that has gone into rural Alaska."

Jim LaBelle believes those feelings emerged partly because of the new economic power Natives had finally attained.

"There was a general backlash, too, in the white community, for having kind of lost its status," LaBelle said. "I always looked at that magazine, the *Alaska Business Monthly,* in the past, as kind of like the good old boys,' pioneers' kind of thing, where they could determine for them, who the 49ers are. Even the name of it. So here, over time, little by little, either through NOLs or the 8(a) program, the Native Corporations started adding their names to that list."

As Alaska's white-owned businesses were sold to national firms and the Native corporations grew, Native corporations took over almost the entire top ten. But the most powerful companies weren't on the list at all, because they weren't Alaska-owned. Alaska's economic landscape was dominated by multinational oil companies.

Today, while teaching university classes, LaBelle says there is plenty of work left to do. Despite owning Alaska's largest corporations, 17 percent of Alaska Natives in Anchorage live in poverty, a higher percentage than any other ethnic group. Cook Inlet Tribal Council, the non-profit Southcentral Foundation and the Alaska Native Tribal Health Consortium have more to do with everyday life for Native residents of Anchorage than do the for-profit corporations. The ANCSA corporations opened the door to Native power, but many organizations and people combined to use that power to change the status of Native people for the better.

Perhaps as a result, the urban-rural divide may be fading. In 2014, the Alaska Legislature added to the official languages of Alaska, including, in addition to English, Iñupiaq, Siberian Yupik, Central Alaskan Yup'ik, Alutiiq, Unangax, Dena'ina, Deg Xinag, Holikachuk, Koyukon, Upper Kuskokwim, Gwich'in, Tanana, Upper Tanana, Tanacross, Han, Ahtna, Eyak, Tlingit, Haida, and Tsimshian.

*Alaska Natives responded to the urban-rural divide with large public marches through downtown Anchorage that expressed strength and unity, shown here in 2001. Photograph by Bill Roth, copyright Alaska Dispatch News.*

# Chapter 11
## Jane Angvik: Unifying Anchorage

Jane Angvik. Copyright Alaska Dispatch News.

Jane Angvik arrived in Anchorage in 1973, short of money but with skills as a community planner in a town that needed them badly. Construction of the trans-Alaska pipeline had begun and the city was spreading across the Anchorage bowl like a spilled cocktail. Young construction workers flowed through the bars with huge paychecks they wanted to blow quickly. It was bigger than the gold rush.

At the Greater Anchorage Area Borough offices on two-lane Tudor Road, Angvik asked the planning director for a job.

"I had worked at a city planning office, I was sitting in front of him, and I could breathe," Angvik recalls. He offered her a salary she could hardly believe. "All I knew was I was going to be able to double my income and come live in a beautiful place that was full of mountains."

Angvik got an apartment with a nurse and a medical records worker. Going out together, they never had to pay for a drink. "We were all 24 or 25, and we'd go to work, and then we'd party all night with all these people who were here to build the pipeline. It was amazing. … This town was wild. It was just bursting. It was really fun."

The average age in Anchorage at the time was 23. Crime, traffic, prostitution and drug abuse spiked. The permissiveness of the disco era hit at the same time as the tsunami of young people with money. City police left for high-paying pipeline jobs. A severe shortage of officers and other workers could be met only with drastic increases in pay and benefits, which also brought double-digit price inflation.

In one year, 1974, the number of vehicles registered in Anchorage increased by 44 percent, hospital admissions rose 79 percent, building permits 35 percent. Robberies went up 65 percent, auto thefts 52 percent. A small one-bedroom apartment rented for over $500, the equivalent of $2,700 today. Local government couldn't cope and the state and federal governments sent emergency financial aid to help.

Older residents bemoaned the loss of the city's small-town feel and the need to lock their doors, just as a previous generation had bemoaned the changes that came with the World War II boom. As in that earlier population rush, newcomers brought new energy and new values and rapidly rose to positions of leadership. Once again, economic opportunities created greater equality. A survey by a Wellesley College sociologist at the time found that women believed they were free to accomplish more without encountering bias in Anchorage than they had been back home.

Angvik was reared in a political household in Minnesota and had worked as a community organizer in a War on Poverty program before coming to Anchorage. As a planner, she jumped into similar work here,

Muldoon Road near the Glenn Highway, a typical 1970s Anchorage street scene. Photograph by Stephen Cysewski, courtesy of the photographer.

taking the new borough mayor, Jack Roderick, to more than 50 community meetings to hear neighborhood concerns. Those meetings became the germ of the community council process that still provides a voice to neighborhoods. The ideas fed into the borough's first comprehensive plan.

In the mid-1950s, the City of Anchorage had marked out greenbelts and a few other lines on the map of the Anchorage bowl beyond city limits. But local government had not existed to plan the majority of the area we now call Anchorage, generally south of Northern Lights Boulevard and east of Merrill Field. When Angvik arrived, all land south of Tudor Road remained unzoned. Without controls, roads blazed by homesteaders became corridors of businesses, strip development. Houses sprouted like mushrooms in the middle of swamps.

"People were coming into the community at the rate of a thousand people a month," Angvik said. "They had no place to sleep, so the marketplace was moving as fast as it could to put up ticky-tacky little houses. … And the challenge was that the planning activity was occurring simultaneously with the development, and the development was being driven much faster by investment than was the planning process."

*A cold day at the Fur Rondy carnival, 1970s. Photograph by Stephen Cysewski, used by permission.*

Conflict exploded weekly at Borough Assembly meetings. Angvik remembers them as screaming matches. They commonly lasted through the night and into the early morning.

The borough had existed for only eight years when Roderick became mayor in 1972. It had never been free of intense controversy. In fact, the people it served had never wanted it at all. With a dysfunctional assembly, a hostile city government, and a new organization, the explosion in growth could not be managed. The Anchorage we live in today reflects those days of chaotic sprawl.

Journalists arrived to see the rush happening in Anchorage, and the reports they sent back were not flattering. Most of Anchorage looked like a dirty highway frontage strip on the edge of any western town: dusty, haphazard and cheap.

"Anchorage is sometimes excused in the name of pioneering," wrote John McPhee in *Coming Into the Country*. "But Anchorage is not a frontier town. It is virtually unrelated to its environment. It has come in on the wind, an American spore. A large cookie cutter brought down on El Paso could lift something like Anchorage into the air."

Like an awkward, acned thirteen-year-old, Anchorage knew it wasn't beautiful, but wasn't sure what to do about the problem. That would come later. That Wellesley professor, Lee Cuba, found that people in Anchorage during the pipeline decade, mostly newcomers, loved being here, felt like real Alaskans, and buzzed with energy and optimism. Many stayed, and as they aged and settled down, the job of making a better city slowly became a community goal. A difficult goal, because of the way it had all started.

The roots of the city's growth problems reached back to its beginnings. Congress prohibited the creation of counties in Alaska during territorial days, presumably to protect the influential fish and mining industries from local taxes. By the time the Alaska Constitutional Convention met in 1955, it didn't want to replicate America's typical local government set-up of cities, towns, and counties, because that produced too many small, overlapping government authorities. The convention's local government committee decided to create a completely new system of local government for Alaska.

Convention delegate Vic Fischer, the Anchorage planner, said the committee sought to make local government as flexible and as powerful as possible, so Alaskans could control their own destiny. An area that wanted maximal local control could form a home rule municipality, which would unify all powers not held by the state government into a single entity. An area that wanted minimal government could choose a regional unit, similar to a county, with towns inside it, and a menu of powers. The committee wanted a new name for this new unit and went through many fanciful choices—tundraburg, poloria, munipuk, and couperie, among others—before settling on borough, which was at least a word in the dictionary.

In Anchorage, local government for the area beyond the city limits was already overdue when statehood arrived in 1959. A USGS report in that year noted that in Spenard, which lacked sewers, closely spaced wells commonly drew water from atop the Bootlegger Cove clay layer, the same aquifer that caught the waste draining down from septic systems. The Spenard Public Utility District, a ten-square-mile area, had its own library, road service, and volunteer fire department, and a private company built a water system there. But across most of the greater Anchorage area, roads were unmaintained, dogs roamed without anyone to catch them, and in case of a fire, it was uncertain if anyone would respond.

Residents outside city boundaries were used to all that. In the late 1950s they resisted being annexed into the city. They showed no interest in being in a borough, either. The constitution drafters had miscalculated when they expected communities to set up boroughs. Three years after statehood, only one small borough had formed, on Bristol Bay.

Without local government, everything became a state issue. Governor Bill Egan noted that he commonly received phone calls, letters and petitions asking him for decisions about filling in a ditch, transferring students to a different school, or prohibiting snake exhibits or junk yards on certain properties. In 1963, he and other state officials lost patience and decided to force Alaska's populated areas to form boroughs.

But the Mandatory Borough Act that passed that year brought outrage, lawsuits and a repeal initiative, which a judge halted as unconstitutional. In Anchorage a group called the Committee for Common Sense Government bought newspaper ads decrying out-of-control big government, bureaucracy and taxation, which it claimed was already choking the area. Residents voted down a proposal to create the Captain Cook Borough for Anchorage by a three-to-one margin in September, 1963. The new state law then automatically created the Greater Anchorage Area Borough on January 1, 1964, with the boundaries of the then-existing election district for the area.

John Asplund became the first borough chairman (equivalent of a mayor), elected to the same position he had held at the Spenard Public Utility District, which the borough absorbed. Asplund focused on building sewers and a sewage treatment plant. Sewage was going underground

*Expansion at the Anchorage International Airport, 1969. Copyright Alaska Dispatch News.*

Construction of the John M. Asplund Sewage Treatment plant, 1971. The battle over the borough's sewers dominated local politics as development spread beyond city limits. Photograph by Steve McCutcheon, courtesy Anchorage Dispatch News.

and into creeks. Sewer systems in the city and on the military bases drained through more than a dozen pipes directly into Cook Inlet.

Debate over sewer construction and city and borough taxes created a level of conflict that is difficult to comprehend 50 years later. Asplund's friends and colleagues remember a man of courage, gentleness and integrity who accomplished a historic step for Anchorage with the sewer system. They said his opponents were self-interested. His opponents, including city government leaders and the powerful *Anchorage Times,* charged that Asplund was a weak manager, too willing to spend on sewers, and ran a poorly functioning local government.

Borough voters supported the sewer project, but its centerpiece took six years of political struggle and 18 lawsuits before it was completed

in 1972. The night before the treatment plant at Point Woronzof was dedicated, the Borough Assembly fulfilled Asplund's hope to have it named after him. He was about to retire.

"There came a time when the citizens of our community decided that living with raw sewage in their neighborhood streams was not tolerable," Asplund said at the ceremony. "We are truly one giant step closer to a clean community with clean air and clean water."

The *Times* congratulated Asplund in an editorial, while again charging him with bungling, confusion and deception. It grudgingly admitted, "Maybe for today the new facility is too much. But few doubt its essential need in the years ahead."

Asplund's project still collects Anchorage's wastewater and puts it through primary treatment, which removes about 75 percent of suspended solids before releasing 58 million gallons a day of liquid through a pipe 800 feet offshore. After 40 years, it is one of only 32 sewage plants nationally not required to treat sewage to a higher level of cleanliness. The Environmental Protection Agency has allowed that situation because Cook Inlet's currents rapidly dilute the water.

Anchorage sewers under construction, 1971. Copyright Alaska Dispatch News.

The sewer system did more to establish the geography of Anchorage than any land use plan. Without sewers, modern health standards require homes to be built on large lots where waste can percolate into the ground. Hillside residents who wanted a rural lifestyle with widely spaced houses stopped sewer extension into their neighborhoods. Since large lots are expensive, that became the most affluent area of town. On the other hand, where sewers went first, housing and businesses were more densely spaced. Those areas ended up as urban neighborhoods.

Sewers also changed the landscape. Bootlegger Cove clay formed a barrier like a sheet of plastic under the ground. Water on top of it filled ponds and swamps all over Anchorage. When water and sewer lines punctured the clay layer, surface water drained away into the soil below, eliminating many wetlands.

The first borough offices stood on Northern Lights Boulevard near the site of today's Barnes and Noble bookstore. Vic Carlson, borough attorney from 1966 to 1969, recalled that he couldn't drive to work on C Street because Blueberry Lake was in the way, a pond used by float planes. C Street stopped at Fireweed Lane and traffic going south jogged over to Barrow Street and threaded through the Arrow Lumber yard (today a bingo hall). But sewer construction broke the clay layer under Blueberry Lake, it drained, and now businesses and offices occupy the space. The only evidence of the lake's existence is the name of Blueberry Road, which connects Fireweed Lane and Northern Lights Boulevard next to Steller Secondary School.

The sewer fight divided the city and borough, but so did urban and rural Alaskan values. The straight, relatively orderly streets of the city, with the library and other public buildings and sewers already in place, came at the cost of higher taxes. Some city residents resented those from outside its boundary who used city facilities without paying city taxes. Those outside the city often saw themselves as rural residents, self-sufficient Alaskans who didn't want government services. To them,

the city threatened too much government and taxes. They wanted to live in Alaska, not Anchorage.

The state law that set up the borough made the conflict worse. The eleven-member Borough Assembly had six of its members elected from outside the city and five chosen from among the membership of the Anchorage City Council. On certain issues, however, each city councilman's vote on the Borough Assembly would be weighted to reflect the population he or she represented. That meant the assembly had five members from the city, but each city member sometimes had 1.4 votes.

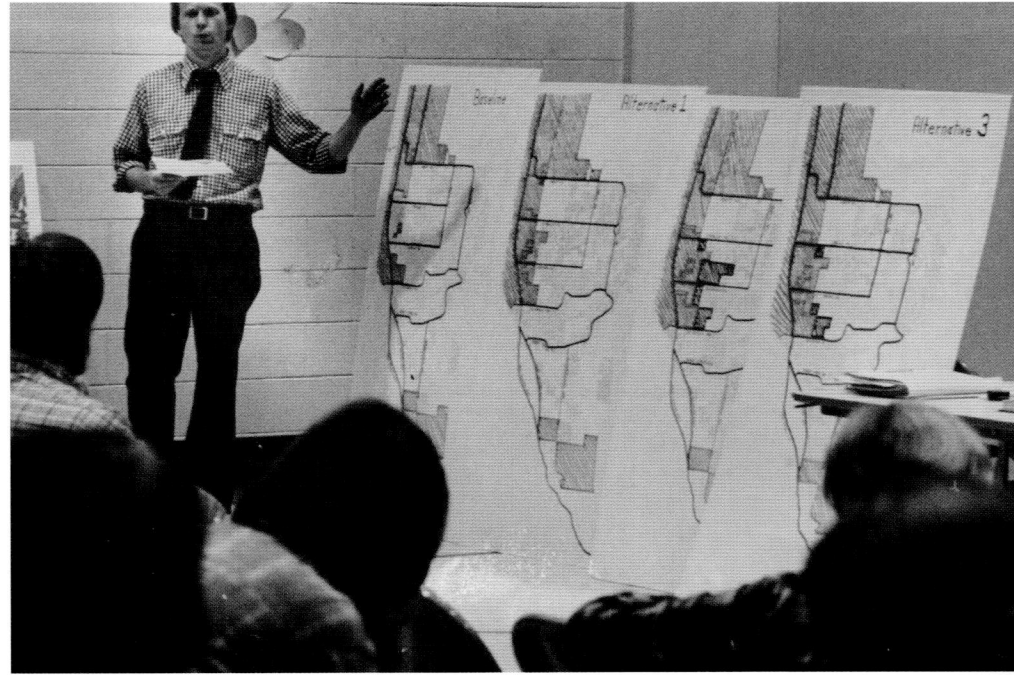

*Sewers and community planning were tightly related as Anchorage mapped out development patterns during its period of rapid growth. Copyright Alaska Dispatch News.*

The Borough Assembly and City Council would meet weekly and pass resolutions criticizing or even suing each other, with five members attending both meetings and voting from both perspectives. The sides voted together, as a bloc, city versus borough. A one-vote switch on any issue made the difference, creating constant temptation for political deals.

Discussions to unify the city and borough began in 1966, and in 1969 a commission was elected to draft a charter for a unified government. It was holding hearings in 1970 when a terrible disaster struck.

*A fire destroyed the Gold Rush Motor Lodge on January, 13, 1970, killing five people, while a city fire truck across the street sat idle because the fire lay outside the city's boundary. The tragedy became a rallying cry for those who wanted to combine the city and borough, but the fight for unification still took five more years. Copyright Alaska Dispatch News.*

The 99-room Gold Rush Motor Lodge caught fire at 2:30 a.m. on the extremely cold night of January 13. The motel stood on the south side of West Northern Lights Boulevard between Dawson and Cheechako streets (the abandoned Northern Lights Inn stands on the same site today). Northern Lights Boulevard formed the city limit. The motor lodge, on the south side, was outside the city, where it had been

built in 1966 without any building code requirements or inspections. It was a fire trap: all wood, without fire walls, alarms or sprinklers. When the borough fire department arrived, within two minutes of the call, half the building was already engulfed in flames and guests trapped in their rooms were screaming from the windows for help.

The city fire department responded, too, but its trucks parked on the far side of the road. City firefighters rushed individually to help the trapped guests. Borough firefighters also requested help from the city's truck to set up an aerial water spray. The city's commander refused, and the truck stood idle across the road while the motel burned. Five people died in the fire.

All the next day on the radio, newsman Herb Shaindlin, a master of outrage and incitement, and a major local voice, built the narrative that the five who had died were victims of the city-borough conflict. A legislative investigation later concluded they would have died even if the city's fire truck had been used. But Shaindlin's version stuck, to be remembered decades later as a turning point in the cause of unification.

At least unification advocates remembered it that way. For years, they called upon the memory of the fire to make their case. But in fact, when the first unification commission's charter came up for a vote the same year, residents outside the city turned it down, despite the fresh memory of the fire. After that defeat, the commission amended the proposal to make it more attractive outside the city, but it failed again in 1971. Asplund and city Mayor George Sullivan tried again with a more limited unification concept in 1972. The Assembly turned it down. Next, the city tried to quit the borough and form its own Cook Inlet Borough. The state turned that down in January 1973. Again that fall, the assembly turned down a new charter commission.

And then the pipeline boom hit. With crime soaring off the charts, the borough had no police department. Alaska State Troopers patrolled the area along with the rest of the state. In 1974, Roderick asked voters for permission to take over the city police department and spread it areawide. A bitter political campaign ensued. Ads paid for by the city government said of the borough, "If they administer the police like they administered the sewers, we'll all go down the drain." The borough government hit back with its own ads accusing the city of dirty campaigning. Taxpayers paid the campaign bills for both sides. The vote failed. Then the city sued the borough for misuse of pipeline impact aid, and taxpayers paid legal fees for both sides of that fight, too.

Jane Angvik had lived in Anchorage only a year when Vic Fischer convinced her to run for the second charter commission in 1974 (he later became her husband). He had been 31 when he attended the constitutional convention; Angvik was 26 when she was elected to the charter commission (Commissioner Lisa Parker, even younger, was still attending Anchorage Community College). The new population of Anchorage was receptive to putting newcomers in charge.

"There is no question that the only reason I was elected was because I was a young, pretty girl," Angvik said. But she had already helped write the borough's first comprehensive plan, working with people in every neighborhood. She saw unification as the only chance for the plan to be implemented. "I had a story about planning, and wanting the community to be better, and I could always talk, and was fearless about that. I don't think it ever occurred to me that I couldn't do it."

Frank Reed, who had lived in Anchorage from its first days, chaired the commission in his warm, courteous style, with a sense of the importance of writing a constitution for the city. Joe Josephson provided the broad view of government and drafted the Bill of Rights. Mary Frohne, a Hillside activist, kept the perspective of the tax-averse, large-lot rural part of Anchorage in view. Arliss Sturgulewski brought together the words.

"Arliss comes from the League of Women Voters," Angvik said. "Arliss believes if you take the notes and write the first draft, you do all the work, you have a much higher probability of influencing the outcome. So Arliss, Shari Holmes, Lisa Parker and I, the women, did that."

Besides creating the basis for a new local government, the commission made some smart decisions to get it approved by voters. One was the service-area concept. Although Anchorage would be one city, areas could opt for the level of service they wanted and were willing to pay for. Another good decision was recognition of the old city's investment of 50 years. In-city residents got a temporary tax break to compensate for the infrastructure they contributed. A third bright idea was having elections for the new mayor and assembly at the same time as the vote on the charter. If the charter didn't pass, those elections for offices would be for nothing, so the candidates campaigned for the charter as well as for themselves.

Before the charter commission was elected, Eagle River and Chugiak had seceded from the borough. But while charter deliberations were going on, a judge ordered the communities back in. That left the commission without any representation from Eagle River or Chugiak, even though those areas would vote on the final document. The commission went to Eagle River to hear the community's concerns. Angvik remembers guns in the audience. As they sat down, each commission member was served with a lawsuit.

"We didn't persuade anyone in Eagle River," Angvik said. But the commission did set up the new Assembly with districts that would allow Eagle River and Chugiak to have its own member (later, the single-member district was moved to downtown and Eagle River and Chugiak got two).

Ground breaking for the Anchorage Baptist Temple in 1976. The city's largest church, led by the conservative Pastor Jerry Prevo, made a deep impression on civic life over the following decade. Copyright Alaska Dispatch News.

Anchorage's new government also pulled in the small town of Girdwood, on Turnagain Arm, without representation on the Charter Commission. Established by gold prospectors in the 1890s, two decades before the first dream of Anchorage's existence, Girdwood had slowly developed with its own government. After gold mining petered out, skiing became Girdwood's reason to exist, and it eventually developed the four-season Alyeska Resort. But when the charter was considered, Girdwood had just a few residents and the community's interests were an afterthought.

On September 9, 1975, voters approved the charter and elected city mayor George Sullivan as mayor of the new unified government over borough mayor Jack Roderick. Six days later, the Greater Anchorage Area Borough ceased to exist and the home rule municipality came into existence, spreading from Eklutna to Portage and east across the Chugach Mountains nearly to Prince William Sound. It was called the Municipality of Anchorage.

The crisis of serving a community in the convulsions of the oil pipeline construction boom continued, and now city leaders also had the job of combining two governments, with two sets of laws, two people in each job, and two sets of labor agreements and financial books. It was an enormous, frustrating task. The Assembly met three times a week, often fighting with Mayor Sullivan. Less than a year after unification, the newspapers reported that the mayor would quit (he didn't).

But the most difficult issue for the new government was completely unexpected: equal rights for gays and lesbians. It had been included by a citizen's committee drafting a law to implement the new charter's Bill of Rights. Mayor Sullivan deleted "sexual preference" from the draft, but the Assembly added it back on a unanimous vote. A gay man, Jim Parsons, had served on the Charter Commission. The next Sunday, an *Anchorage Times* article noted how uncontroversial the change had been.

That day, a brand new force erupted on the scene: Christian conservatives led by Dr. Jerry Prevo of the Anchorage Baptist Temple. They flooded Assembly members, the mayor and the newspapers with angry messages demanding the ordinance be vetoed or repealed.

The issue gripped the community for the first three months of 1976, with at least two Assembly meetings drawing unruly crowds of nearly 1,000 people, the largest ever seen. The gay rights proposal died under Mayor Sullivan's veto, only to be proposed again, with similarly intense opposition, in 1993, 2009 and 2012. Today the vast majority of Americans live under equal rights laws for gays and lesbians, but not in Anchorage or Alaska as a whole.

In 1976, that opposition came as a surprise for local politicians. Before the pipeline years, no giant churches existed in Anchorage. Social issues didn't produce much heat: Alaska abolished the death penalty in 1957, legalized abortion in 1970, added the right to privacy to the state constitution in 1972, and decriminalized small amounts of marijuana in 1975. Anchorage's gay rights fight of 1976 was the first time church members had flexed political muscle. But in the decades after, Prevo and Christian conservatives shaped much of the political debate on social issues.

Pipeline construction ended in 1977. Growth slowed, but the city had gained a new size, a new identity, and enough new, young people to transform the population. Memories of the Greater Anchorage Area Borough rapidly faded away, although the service area system still allows neighborhoods to customize the level of government they want. For example, Eagle River and Chugiak still don't have a building code.

But more boom-time development was on the horizon.

*Skiers double-pole past Westchester Lagoon, 2004. Photograph by Bob Hallinen, copyright Alaska Dispatch News.*

# Chapter 12

## Connie Yoshimura:
## The Last Boom and Bust

Connie Yoshimura. Photo courtesy of Yoshimura.

Connie Yoshimura didn't plan to become wealthy in real estate and probably no one expected her to. New to town in 1979, living in a basement apartment in Spenard without friends, family or other connections, with experience mainly waiting tables, she had never been inside a single family house in Anchorage until the first time she showed one to a prospective buyer. She wasn't a glad-handing salesperson: she was a poet with a first-class education in creative writing, who went through graduate school without once speaking up in class. She began selling houses so she could earn enough money to quit and write poetry.

*Cranes constantly grew the Anchorage skyline in 1982. The economic boom erased wood frame houses built during quieter times and replaced them with glass and steel structures. Photograph by Paul Brown, copyright* Alaska Dispatch News.

But a lot of improbable things happened in Anchorage in the 1980s. In 1979, an Islamic revolution took over Iran and seized the American embassy in Tehran. That caused world oil prices to spike to levels never before imagined. At the same time, the new trans-Alaska pipeline ramped up to full throughput. Money flowed into the state treasury at a mind-boggling rate. Although huge sums were saved in the Alaska Permanent Fund, the legislature still spent so much it super-heated the economy with a frenzy of capital projects and loan programs.

Nationally, economic times were hard. Mortgage interest rates peaked above 17 percent and the construction industry suffered. In Alaska, everything was different. The state subsidized various kinds of loans. Mortgage rates were held down as much as five percent below the going national rate. The state invested $1 billion in the Alaska Housing Finance Corporation to give those loans, and AHFC borrowed billions more through financial markets to lend out to Alaskans at low rates.

Alaska imported thousands of construction workers to build its new roads and civic buildings, and imported more workers to build homes for the new residents to live in. New arrivals boosted the population, as did a baby boom, as the batch of newcomers who had arrived during pipeline construction settled down and had children. Housing was in demand and prices were rising. The effect was bigger in the Anchorage area than anywhere else in Alaska. There was a lot of money to be made building and selling houses and shopping centers.

Yoshimura had set off from home and college in Iowa to learn about the world with the goal of being a better writer. She did that in the hippy culture of San Francisco, then followed a boyfriend to Anchorage. Here she found exploding economic opportunity and a frontier culture that was relatively open to a woman in business. She had to fight to overcome the social barriers of her gender, her fluctuating weight, and her Japanese-American heritage, but she believes those fights were winnable here, as they might not have been somewhere else.

When she arrived, she still thought of herself as a waitress. But like many who arrived for the boom of the '80s, she found opportunities in Anchorage she had never considered before. And she had the requisite qualities for success, the same ones a poet needs: drive and good ideas.

"I am a good example of what can happen to you if you hit it just right," Yoshimura said. But she was much more than lucky. She had an extraordinary aptitude for selling houses, something she realized in her first month on the job. "It really seemed just sort of like a natural thing. And I didn't know anything about houses. … You don't have to have a lot of knowledge in order to begin a career selling real estate. Knowledge is something you can acquire easily. But you do have to have a fair amount of intuition about people. About what motivates them."

Without contacts to help her develop a list of clients, she concentrated on selling houses for homebuilders. She won builders' trust by going to job sites early in the morning, like their subcontractors, and she added value to their work by sharing trends about housing styles she picked up at seminars. She built her profile by writing a newspaper column about real estate. And she worked very hard. In 1983, she sold $22 million in property in a single year.

In a picture of Yoshimura from that time she wears fur. She left Spenard and moved to a luxurious condominium in the downtown Peterson Towers, and then she built a 5,200-square-foot house in tony Resolution Pointe in South Anchorage. To live in all by herself.

She remembers her friend Howard Weaver, editor of the *Anchorage Daily News,* saying, "You're never going to be a writer, Connie, living in a big house like this."

It all happened astonishingly fast. Rick Mystrom, a member of the Anchorage Assembly at the time, recalled how the price of oil rose from $3 a barrel when pipeline construction began in 1973 to $14 a barrel when it was finished in 1977, and then to $37 a barrel in 1980. That's $106 in today's dollars, and the pipeline was handling about three times as much oil as it does today.

"The state was awash with money at $30 a barrel," Mystrom said. "And I remember George Sullivan having a work session he called with the Assembly, in which he said Governor Hammond and the legislature want to give each community in Alaska $1,000 dollars per person per year for the next three years for capital projects, and we need to have an answer for them in two months about what we are going to do with this money.

"We had to tell them what we wanted to do with this $250 million Anchorage was going to get each year for three years, and that's over and above all the normal capital projects, the police buildings, and fire, and everything else. It's not instead of, it's over and above that. Just what different things, what additional things do you want to do?"

Mayor Sullivan rapidly put together a list of five major projects, any one of which could have challenged a community under normal circumstances, buildings which became the Egan Convention Center, the Sullivan Arena, the Loussac Library, an Anchorage Museum expansion, and the Alaska Center for the Performing Arts. He called the package Project 80s.

Plenty of controversy would surround individual projects. The convention center was built on the city's town square block, over the objections of park advocates. The park ultimately moved a block south to its current location, after the city bought and demolished businesses there. The library was designed to have a parking structure, but the state's largesse ran out before money was appropriated for it, leaving the building with an impractical second-floor entry that had been intended to meet the level of the garage. The performing arts center went drastically over budget, got withering reviews for its decoration, and had chronic roof problems.

But the doubts and frustrations came later. The decision to launch the projects was easy. Local leaders felt the money had simply fallen in their laps and needed to be spent quickly.

"There was no discussion about whether we should take it or not take it," Mystrom said. The financial benefit was beyond questioning. "Some city our size may have a better library or a better sports arena. But no city our size has all five of those things. And certainly no city our size has all five of those things and no debt. There was never any debt we had to repay on those things. No general obligation bonds at all. We just built them."

Sullivan left office in 1981 after 14 years in office, which he served first with the city and then the unified municipality, by far the longest service of any mayor of Anchorage. He probably could have continued to win elections, but the 1975 charter limited him to two three-year terms. Project 80s allowed Sullivan to extend his priorities beyond his time in office. Most of the work remained to be done.

Mayor Tony Knowles shared Sullivan's interest in improving the appearance and amenities of Anchorage—most mayors did—but he came from a new generation. Sullivan had been an Alaskan pioneer and a working man, a trucker and U.S. Marshal, and never attended college. He looked like the old-time Irish politician he was, with a big face that filled with creases when he smiled, a quick sense of humor, and consummate skill in working a room. Knowles looked better on TV. He was athletic, handsome and had a degree from Yale. With his Oklahoma accent and oil industry background, he shared qualities with the migrants who had populated Anchorage after Prudhoe Bay.

Knowles also differed from Sullivan on social issues. His 1981 election campaign surged when he refused to respond to a questionnaire from the Moral Majority, a national Christian conservative group connected locally with Dr. Jerry Prevo, who had backed Sullivan's opposition to gay rights.

But Knowles was eager to finish Sullivan's work on the Project 80s buildings. "These were fundamental," he said. "If you're going to be a modern city that embraces the entire community, these are important facilities to have."

The wave of state money was only starting when Knowles came to office, and he added many more ideas to the list. The biggest project of his two terms was the $180 million Eklutna Water project, which solved the city's water needs for generations, with a treatment plant at Eklutna Lake and a pipeline to bring the water to Anchorage. The city also doubled the size of the Asplund Sewage Treatment Plant, built a modern landfill, accelerated its road construction program by four times, built a police station, two fire stations, a homeless shelter, a transit facility and a port headquarters, and assisted in development of the Fifth Avenue Mall downtown, constructing an adjoining parking garage and demolishing a row of bars and other buildings to make way for upscale shopping.

Knowles became best known for beautification and parks and trails. Skinny trees and tiny bushes newly planted along roads would, after years of growth, soften the city's harsh, dusty edge. Three recreation centers, a ski chalet, an indoor ice rink, a golf course and equestrian center. And 44 kilometers of ski trails, 12 miles of running trails, 34 miles of bike trails, all topped with the 10-mile coastal trail, which the Assembly named for Knowles as he left office. It had likewise named the arena for Sullivan who also received a lifetime pass to events there.

People liked the improvements. What city would turn down the money to build all its dream projects at once? But spending so much money so quickly created an economic hazard. Mystrom, who was investing in buildings with income from his successful advertising business, started to notice pages being added to the apartment-for-rent classified ads in the newspaper. Connie Yoshimura had sold some of her rentals and used the proceeds to start her own real estate agency and kept earning commissions. Despite a softening market, construction and lending continued at a rapid pace.

Dan Cuddy, the president of First National Bank of Anchorage, realized something was wrong with a real estate market driven by an economy that was itself driven by construction and real estate. "You had carpenters building houses for carpenters," he said. "In '83 we decided we weren't going to have any more of that, and it took until '84 to get it cleaned up."

Oil prices peaked in 1981, but spending by the legislature kept rising until 1985. Subdivisions and condominium developments sprawled into instant neighborhoods. Strip malls popped up everywhere. The housing stock increased by 40 percent. With AHFC making all the mortgage loans, some banks turned to aggressive lending to developers buying land and building streets, utilities and houses.

"I had one loan officer tell me once, 'We don't really care about the project, we only care about the financial statement and the creditworthiness of the client,'" Yoshimura said. "Well, that bank no longer exists. Because you can't lend millions of dollars without believing in the project itself."

Alaska Bank of Commerce, that bank, was one of fourteen Alaska banks and savings and loans that would fail during the 1980s.

Alaska, and especially Anchorage, was in a classic investment bubble, said economist Scott Goldsmith, of the UAA Institute of Social and Economic Research. But that was much easier to see in retrospect.

Fourteen banks and savings and loans failed during the Alaska crash of the 1980s. Late in 1987, Forest Paulson uncovers the sign for the new Alliance Bank, created by federal insurers out of the failed Alaska Mutual and United Bank Alaska, but Alliance itself failed less than two years later. Photograph by Bob Hallinen, copyright Alaska Dispatch News.

"I think the feeling was that it was not a boom so much as the new reality," Goldsmith said. "It was just hard for people to see that things could slow down. They didn't want to see it. Certainly people didn't want to talk about it. As long as things are growing, you want to be in on the action. You don't want to be left behind. People always think they're smart enough to be able to pull out when things start turning down. But of course it happens so quickly. Everybody tried to pull out at once, and only a few were lucky enough to escape unscathed."

The party ended in 1985. Oil prices dropped. The oil industry began laying off workers. But the state government, distracted by impeachment hearings against Governor Bill Sheffield, postponed action. In 1986, oil prices fell much more, to a third of what they had been at the peak. Sheffield used his veto power to cancel the entire capital construction plan for the state, laid off hundreds of state workers, cut pay and slashed revenue payments to communities, which began laying off their own employees. Yet state spending still exceeded expected revenue by 40 percent when he left office at the end of the year. After a five-year spending binge, Alaska was going cold turkey.

The economy stopped in its tracks, beginning with the construction industry and housing market. A thousand people a month left Anchorage for two straight years; during the crash, the population dropped by 10 percent. Bankruptcy court was flooded with new filings. Single-family housing prices in Anchorage dropped 25 percent on average, and condos 50 percent. In 1987, Anchorage had 14,000 vacant housing units and 7 percent of mortgages were in foreclosure. Some owners simply abandoned their homes and left the keys in the mailbox.

Yoshimura recalled that the Foxwood Condos in Midtown had sold for $76,000. When AHFC raised the amount it would loan to buyers, the price matched the program, jumping to $82,500. In the crash, the units dropped to $32,000. (Now they sell for around $140,000.) Some condos sold for under $20,000 at big government auctions. Agencies ended up owning many low-quality units that wouldn't sell at any price; they were demolished or converted to other uses. Some vacant shopping centers were cut up and trucked off to find another purpose.

Many who lived here at the time remember the weird feeling of driving through vacant subdivisions where all the houses seemed to be abandoned or never occupied. A city whose skyline had been choked with cranes became utterly still. Heavy equipment had been everywhere and now was nowhere. The rare sight of a working yellow loader felt as hopeful as the first flower of spring.

In 1987, one of Goldsmith's ISER reports said, "We'll know the Alaska recession is over when we can open a newspaper and see no mention of layoffs or banks on the brink of failure; when we go to a store we haven't been to in six months and find it still in business; when we can drive around and see no notices for garage sales that say: 'Everything Must Go—Leaving State.'"

With so many people losing jobs, businesses and homes, bankruptcy and default lost its social stigma. Some bankers and developers were prosecuted for illegal lending that came to light after financial collapse, but more changed careers or left the state and to start again. Tens of thousands of Alaskans lost everything. Yoshimura lost money when she sold her rentals, but repaid her banks and kept her business.

*Equipment digs the foundation of the Fifth Avenue Mall in the summer of 1986. Photograph by Michael Penn, copyright Alaska Distpatch News.*

Her office was a sad place. Agents felt guilty for having sold properties at the top of the market. "We all had golden chains around our necks, and we were all really, really depressed," she said.

She hired new agents. She needed people who saw low prices as opportunities rather than failures.

The downturn created huge opportunities. Yoshimura's firm helped sell AHFC's inventory of foreclosed houses, which numbered in the thousands. She bought home sites in bulk from the Federal Deposit Insurance Corp. and sold them immediately for as much as twice what she paid. She started a property management business to take care of vacant units. She even began developing a new residential area, Kempton Park, with partners.

The economy stopped losing jobs in 1988. In 1989, the *Exxon Valdez* oil spill added thousands of short-term cleanup jobs; six percent of households had at least one member working on the spill. Although that activity ended quickly, it probably created business confidence that the slump would end, a kind of psychological closure. But in 1990, 30 percent of Anchorage homeowners still owed more on their houses than the houses were worth.

Slow, steady growth continued for almost three decades, until the national economic downturn of 2008. Was the crash of 1985 the last bust in Anchorage's boom-and-bust cycle? Economists can't predict the future accurately or say why something didn't happen in the past, but there are several explanations of why the city entered a new economic pattern. The crash taught business people valuable lessons and purged the economy of excess. Larger tourism and air freight industries diversified the job market. No more massive resource projects came along.

Most importantly, state spending became more stable. Under governors Steve Cowper and Walter Hickel, the state amended its constitution to save rather than spend sudden windfalls of money, and then

The state's windfall of oil money in the early 1980s paid for many projects to expand and modernize roads, such as Providence Drive, and powered an unsustainable economic boom. Copyright Alaska Dispatch News.

those savings accounts were filled with enormous oil tax settlement payments. The saved funds cushioned the bad years and were replenished when oil prices rose again many years later.

A popular bumper sticker in the 1980s said, "Please God, let there be another oil boom. I promise not to piss it all away next time." Cowper and Hickel helped prevent a repeat. But were the oil booms of the 1970s and 1980s truly wasted in Anchorage?

In the depths of the city's economic depression, the belief became common that the good times had been a wasteful party. Goldsmith's work at ISER showed how excessive state spending had drawn migrants to Alaska, many of whom left as soon as the music stopped. Services, facilities and payments to support those temporary Alaskans consumed 28 percent of the new state spending. "How dumb is that?" he asked.

But the facilities remained. The state had spent money on many failed projects during the boom years, most notably a massive agriculture program that paid for farms, rail cars, grain terminals, cows and everything else, producing a harvest of financial ruin. In Anchorage, however, the investments of the 1980s under Sullivan and Knowles are still in use. They bring our water, house our meetings and cultural activities, allow us to move across town, and even give us an attractive place to shop. Anchorage's nationally recognized trails have become a defining characteristic of the city. Even the housing crisis modernized and improved the housing stock. Every day, every Anchorage resident uses buildings and projects from the 1980s boom.

Connie Yoshimura attained considerable wealth during those years, and maintained and added to it in the years that followed. But along with the city's mixed story of waste and accomplishment, her own experience carried enduring questions.

She had lived her Iowa childhood unhappy and abused, but redeemed it through her writing talent. She won a fellowship at the Iowa Writer's Workshop, the nation's most famous creative writing program, where she worked with novelist Kurt Vonnegut. But she'd never seen the ocean. When she graduated, Vonnegut, who towered above her, patted her on the head and said, "What you need, little girl, is to go out and experience the world."

But was she still following Vonnegut's advice? She did experience the world. She married three times. But did she squander her writing talent on the distraction of business? She believes the real estate column she wrote every week damaged her skill as a writer. But she also wrote five plays that explored deep issues about her traumas, encouraged by Out North Theater, a community art house started in 1985 by a pair of gay men to explore cutting-edge artistic issues. Her money allowed her to travel to writing workshops outside Alaska and therapy when she wanted to.

"The only regret that I have is that I haven't done more writing. It's a skill and you lose it," she said. "My whole goal always was to make enough money to quit and write books. I guess 30 years later that is still my goal, but I have found that the work that I do in real estate is still a very creative process. And it is hard to leave it behind.

"You know, writers are poor. I was poor, and I didn't want to be poor."

Indra Arriaga. She created the sculpture "We've come so far" with Christina Barber. Photograph courtesy of Arriaga.

# Chapter 13

## *Indra Arriaga: Cultural Intersections*

A trio of large concrete figures stands in front of the McDonald's restaurant on Mountain View Drive, in the most ethnically diverse census tract in the nation. Each red figure is carved by many cuts and wrapped loosely with a heavy rope. They stand together, but it isn't clear which direction they are facing, or how they are related. They might be a family.

Indra Arriaga and Christina Barber were living together when they conceived of the piece, thinking about proposing a public art work as part of the community's revitalization in 2008.

"We were having dinner, and drinking, and it just kind of happened," Arriaga said. "It was born out of somebody who is four-generation Alaskan, American, with her own story. And then my concept."

Arriaga's ideas reflect the diversity within her. She is a citizen of Mexico and the United States who has made her home in Alaska but thinks of herself as Mexican. A research analyst formerly in the securities industry and now in policy and research work, and a painter and sculptor who thinks of herself first as an artist. A bisexual woman whose roots and home base remain in a Mexican town where traditional values rule.

In Anchorage, she fits in. Over the last two decades, a city that once seemed as monochromatic as a glass of milk has swirled with international colors. In this cloud of different kinds of people, the typical resident may be one who is herself a collection of influences.

The women named the piece, "We've come from so far."

Arriaga said, "No matter where you're from, whether you're from the Bush, or whether you're from one neighborhood or another, or whether you are from Samoa, or the Philippines, or Russia, or Norway, or Mexico, or other parts of Latin America, you're coming from so far, and sometimes the distance is not just physical, it's emotional, it's political, it's social."

Some people didn't like the sculpture. They saw blood where Arriaga saw the earthy red clay of her native Veracruz. They saw bondage in the ropes and violence in the cuts. Arriaga was OK with that. The immigrant experience does leave scars and bonds, which can be painful. Or the scars can mark each of us as unique, and the bonds can be the securing ties to family and home.

Arriaga said, "You can't get rid of your ties, no matter how hard you try, but they're loose enough that you can create new ties. That's the heart of the piece."

The story of how Anchorage became so diverse is different for each individual who came, but the fact that it happened in a single generation reflects the city's success. After the economy stabilized following the booms of the 1970s and '80s, the mostly white migrants from that era settled down and had kids. But as the number of people born here steadily rose, Anchorage also continued attracting America's most ambitious and mobile populations—immigrants and their children—because it is an attractive place to live.

"It is the cleanest city, compared to the Lower 48," said Arthur Yang, a leader in the Hmong community. "Not so crowded, traffic, and everything. So people move here for the weather, the clean city, and the better opportunity, like employment."

Yang was born in Laos and recruited at age 12 from a school yard to fight in the Viet Nam War on the American side. After the war, the Hmong were ejected from their homeland and gained entry to the U.S. as refugees. Yang first lived in Minneapolis, joining the Hmong community that formed in Anchorage after forerunners sent word of what they had found here.

"We are stable here," Yang said. "People move here for economic opportunities. Hmong, here, are working. Mom working day, Dad working night, they are working for low wages, but working very hard."

Yang and other minority residents still encounter prejudice, but many feel Anchorage is more accepting of differences than other places they have lived.

"You know, I go to some other places, and they stay with their own kind, and you do not see smiles on their faces," said Elsa Sargento, a leader in the Filipino community who came to Anchorage in 1974. "Here in Anchorage, here in Alaska, smile, and you get a smile back. It really is true."

In 1960, only eight percent of Anchorage residents were non-white. In 1980, 16 percent. In 2010, 34 percent. Sargento said Anchorage has gotten more comfortable for her over the years as her English improved. Japanese-American business person Connie Yoshimura said she feels better here now than in the all-white community she encountered in 1979, and the food is better. Native leader Jim LaBelle said he lived in Anchorage more than 20 years before he felt he belonged. Getting to know members of other minorities, as they became more numerous, made the difference.

At times, the change has been difficult. In January, 1986, a citizens' committee asked the Anchorage Assembly to rename Ninth Avenue for Dr. Martin Luther King, Jr., at the same time as the national holiday was established in his honor. Strong opposition developed from residents who said the name would be inconvenient or would disrupt the system of numbered streets, or that King didn't deserve the honor. The Assembly never voted on the idea.

"I believe if it was going to be named Ronald Reagan Parkway, we'd have had out the caviar and wine," committee member Delilah Williams told a reporter. "People didn't want to live on a street that was named after a black man."

Embarrassed about the racial implications of their avoided decision, the Assembly asked a follow-up committee to find something else to name for King. It recommended the new performing arts center. The debate lasted nine months. Opponents argued that King didn't have enough connection to Alaska, or to the arts. Assembly members were deluged with calls and letters, including some expressing extreme racism. Assembly member John Wood ripped up a racist letter he had received as a public demonstration at an Assembly meeting.

Paul Connerty, executive director of the Anchorage Equal Rights Commission, said at the time, "We don't have the presence of the Ku Klux Klan, but there certainly are some things that suggest we are a fertile ground for that kind of activity. This issue brought that kind of sentiment up to the surface. We can't close our eyes to the fact we have problems here."

In September, 1986, the Assembly voted 10-1 to name the center for King. But former Assembly member and legislator Don Smith raised a petition drive to overturn the naming. When the election came, a year later, the public stripped King's name from the center by a 3-1 margin. National media highlighted the vote as a sign of racial attitudes in Alaska.

*After a 1980s controversy in which voters stripped Dr. Martin Luther King's name from the city's performing arts center, Anchorage has found various ways to honor his civil rights legacy, including a monument on the Delaney Park Strip, shown here in January, 2014. Photograph by Erik Hill, copyright Alaska Dispatch News.*

The center opened with the name Alaska Center for the Performing Arts. The Anchorage School District named its job skills center for King, and, decades later, a new road in east Anchorage became Dr. Martin Luther King Jr. Avenue. A Delaney Park Strip monument dedicated to King in 1998 explains the history of civil rights in Alaska, connecting King's message with the legacy of the struggle for equality here. Supporters said that the monument, placed without controversy, and built with donated funds, permanently settled the question of why King's name is important to Alaska.

Anchorage changed in the 1990s. Communications to the outside world became frictionless with telephone competition and the Internet. Airline competition drove down the cost of getting to Anchorage. And large national retailers discovered the city. Big box stores appeared as if at the click of a mouse from some unseen corporate headquarters. Brand-name hotels went up throughout Midtown, seemingly overnight.

These new employers added thousands of lower-wage retail and hospitality jobs and offered lower prices. Anchorage pay and prices had always been higher than Outside. Now that gap narrowed.

Anchorage's leaders had worked from the start to connect the city to the Outside, to make it as much a part of America as possible. As the city matured, barriers between Anchorage and the rest of the U.S. dissolved. Recent immigrants tend to move frequently, looking for the best spot to raise their families. With about a tenth of the population cycling in and out every year, the proportion of minorities in Anchorage kept rising.

Indra Arriaga came to Anchorage with her first wife to help care for her wife's dying mother, found a good consulting job, and decided to stay. She had never planned to go to Anchorage. She had grown up waiting tables in her parents' neighborhood restaurant in San Antonio, Texas, and also in Xalapa, Mexico, where she was part of their warm extended families.

Mayor Rick Mystrom joins other members of Bridge Builders of Anchorage in reciting a pledge of mutual respect at a Martin Luther King Jr. Holiday Celebration at West High School in 2013. West is among the three most diverse high schools in the United States; the other two are Anchorage's East and Bartlett highs. Photograph by Erik Hill, Alaska Dispatch News.

"At the restaurant one of the regulars was a friend of my father's who was a painter," she recalled. "He said to me one day, 'You know, you're 15, you're smart, you're going to get in trouble. Maybe you should paint.' I said, 'Ok, sure.' So we went and we bought acrylics and a canvas and he walked me though my first painting."

Arriaga left home for education, for art, and for freedom. She still connected with her parents at home, but she sensed they didn't understand her work as an artist or the financial and technical work she did to support it, and she didn't tell them for many years about her girlfriends. Anchorage represented another step toward possibilities. Art here could be created without limits, outside of tradition.

"It has a lot of room to just branch out into whatever," she said. "So that's why I stayed. The job was really interesting. There was an opportunity to make art. The community is really tight, and really nice, and I've made some really good friends. And being part of this emerging Latin culture has been really fun, too."

The mixing of races and ethnicities is a unique aspect of Anchorage's diversity. Other cities have a larger percentage of minorities, and Anchorage's 34 percent minority population is only somewhat higher than the nation as a whole (28 percent). But few cities are as integrated as Anchorage, with many ethnic and racial groups of significant size living together, including Natives and whites, groups that are absent in minority neighborhoods in most American cities.

Mountain View and the area around it is the most diverse residential neighborhood in the United States, with Muldoon, Russian Jack, Spenard and Midtown not far behind, according to census calculations by UAA sociologist Chad Farrell. Some Anchorage neighborhoods are much less integrated, but diversity is rarely far away. Anchorage is a patchwork, with affluent areas next to low-income areas, partly because of the way much of the city grew without effective community planning. Well-off Turnagain is 87 percent white, but children from Turnagain attend the third most diverse high school in the nation, West High. The most diverse in the U.S. is East High and the second is Bartlett High.

By the mid-1990s, the change in Anchorage's population was evident. It brought conflict and youth crime among minority groups. But good-hearted efforts also developed to bridge the divides.

In February, 1996, Rev. David Bleivik of the First Presbyterian Church, a congregation of old Anchorage families, proposed to swap pulpits and choirs for a Sunday with Rev. Alonzo Patterson, of the mostly African-American Shiloh Baptist Church. Patterson had previously preached to Catholic and Jewish congregations in town and pulpit swaps were happening across the country. An *Anchorage Daily News*

article about the event caught the attention of Mayor Rick Mystrom, who invited both pastors for dinner at his home in Turnagain to discuss how to improve race relations in Anchorage.

Out of that dinner came the idea for Bridge Builders, Mystrom's initiative to create understanding and respect among Anchorage's cultures one person at a time. Members of different ethnic groups were matched to one another for dinners at home and friendship, with a commitment to spend a year doing activities together. A simple idea that seemed nice, but perhaps not enough to change a city.

But Bridge Builders exploded in popularity, with hundreds of people coming out to potluck dinners to be matched, and the group became a self-sustaining non-profit organization involving as many as 43 cultures. A booklet explained the etiquette of each culture from the point of view of its own members to make the meetings more comfortable. The group adopted the goal of making Anchorage the first city without prejudice.

In 1997, a group of eleven Samoan chiefs and reverends came to Mystrom's office to apologize for a series of shootings involving young Samoan men. Mystrom assigned his aide, Malcolm Roberts, who had helped start Bridge Builders, to work with the Samoans and other minority groups to reduce youth crime. Roberts and United Way executive director Dennis McMillian dove into the work, attending many meetings where they didn't understand the language. Roberts became the most familiar establishment face in the city's minority communities. Mystrom said they called him, "Mr. Malcolm, the assistant mayor."

Bridge Builders did encounter difficulties, Mystrom said, such as when the cultural groups wanted to march in the city's Fourth of

July parade. "I got a lot of negative comments from people saying this is an American thing. This is for America," Mystrom said. "And my reaction was, these people are as American or more American than I am. I am only a second generation American. My grandparents came from Sweden. It's just that I look the same as all the other Caucasians so that nobody can tell. And so we got past that, and I think we may have won some converts, and we may have quieted down those people who are not going to convert."

Roberts worked with the Samoan and Tongan communities, traditionally bitter enemies on their home islands, to put together a joint float with the leaders of both on board. The same day as the parade, photographs of the float made it to Polynesia and messages returned to Anchorage with reactions of amazement and congratulation.

Students of the Somos Amigos Spanish Academy perform at an event to celebrate the city's diversity called "Meet the World in Anchorage," which was held at the Anchorage Museum in 2005. Photograph by Erik Hill, Alaska Dispatch News.

Alaska's minority communities began to gather political and economic power. The urban-rural divide of the 1990s brought Natives to the streets to protest, as described in chapter 10. After the Alaska Federation of Natives moved its huge annual convention to Fairbanks, Anchorage put on a vigorous campaign to win it back.

In the final weeks of his campaign for the U.S. Senate in 2008, Mayor Mark Begich welcomed AFN to the city in a new convention center. He told the delegates, "We have tried to erase the urban-rural divide by putting Anchorage on the side of rural Alaska."

The center was the first major new civic building in Anchorage since the completion of the performing arts center that had been briefly named for Martin Luther King Jr. Begich reminded the delegates that, at one time, businesses had posted signs that said, "No dogs or Natives," but now the city had named the new center for the Dena'ina.

"Not only are those offensive signs gone, but now we've put up a new sign that declares our grandest showplace is named for the Native people of our region," Begich said.

Begich's administration also invested heavily in the Mountain View neighborhood, designating it an art and culture district and building office space for non-profit groups, as well as funding a new library and bike trail, assisting development of a shopping center, and installing road improvements and amenities, including Arriaga's sculpture. The Cook Inlet Housing Authority and Habitat for Humanity built new single-family housing scattered through the neighborhood.

Mountain View remains a low-income area, but it's not a slum or ghetto. It has improved noticeably over the last 20 years. But news reports of violent crimes still seem to originate more from there than from other areas. Despite extra federal funding, performance in the schools in Mountain View lags behind average on standardized tests.

Many students come to school lacking strong English and with other challenges. The Anchorage School District serves children with 95 different primary languages spoken at home.

Some residents believe the cost of schooling the city's mix of ethnicities is too high. In response, Mayor Dan Sullivan attended a news conference in 2014 to declare, "All are welcome in Anchorage," and the great majority of people in public life express similar sentiments. But not all. No one claims that the Bridge Builders goal of making Anchorage the first city without prejudice has been achieved. The reported experience of minority members in Anchorage suggests that most people accept the city's new colors, but not everyone.

*A teen mariachi band representing musicians of several races practices regularly in Indra Arriaga's art studio. Photograph courtesy of Arriaga.*

The ethnic experience in Anchorage is new and still evolving. A teenaged mariachi band practices in Arriaga's large art studio above a transmission shop off Arctic Boulevard. She said many of the players have never been to Mexico but are looking for a link to an identity as a Mexican.

"They're not all Mexican, because frankly there aren't enough Mexicans here, especially who are musicians," she said. "So you've got African American kids and Asian kids. … They reflect Anchorage really nicely."

Arriaga looks completely typical walking on the Tony Knowles Coastal Trail on a warm spring evening, a small, brown woman with intelligent eyes and short, tidy hair. Runners, cyclists and other pedestrian pass by and smile at her two little dogs, a Westie and Yorkie, who investigate the ground and tangle their leashes. But she has experienced racial prejudice, both by being made to feel invisible, and by being challenged as a suspicious person—even outside her own condo in an affluent area.

She said she doesn't take the time to worry about it.

"I feel the best way for me to fight racism, or be whatever it is I am, is just to be it. So when I think of my neighbors, they may not like me because of my race, they may not like me because of my sexuality, they may not like me because I am an artist. I have no idea why they may or may not like me, but my job is to be visible. And if I am visible, that is a more positive way of making change."

# Chapter 14

## Dan Sullivan and Mark Begich: The Alaska-Grown Generation

Mark Begich as a young man at the dedication of the monument to his father, Nick, in the Congressional Cemetery, in the late 1970s. Nick died when a campaign flight disappeared in 1972. Mark was 10 years old at the time. Photograph courtesy of the Begich family.

For its first five years, Anchorage was governed by federal officials and didn't have a mayor. Over the next 83 years, the city had 30 mayors, some of whom spent their lives here, but none of whom were originally from Anchorage. For almost 12 years, Anchorage had two mayors, one for the city and one for the borough. But only in 2003 did Anchorage elect a mayor who had been born here, Mark Begich. And, in 2009, the next mayor elected was from Anchorage, too, Dan Sullivan.

Begich and Sullivan are from opposite parties and opposite sides of town. They have been determined political adversaries. But both men are products of Anchorage, of its public schools, its peaceful neighborhoods, and its vigorous politics; of its fast economic growth, booming opportunities, and sudden setbacks; of its open frontier culture, in which people are judged on what they do currently rather than where they came from; of its mountains, as seen on a winter morning, sharply silhouetted in a pink sunrise. Moreover, they are both the sons of leaders and learned about public service around the family dinner table.

It would be a surprise if these two men had nothing in common, and in fact their visions for the city as mayor have been remarkably similar. Both saw quality of life as key to Anchorage's economic health and sought to improve the aspects that draw people to live and locate businesses here. Both saw Anchorage as a headquarters and as an international city. Other mayors expressed the same ideas. Despite the daily struggle of politics, the basic direction of those leading Anchorage has persisted for generations.

*Margaret Sullivan, her son Dan, and husband George. The photograph was taken at Dan's wedding to Lynnette in 1985. Photograph courtesy of the Sullivan family.*

Sullivan said, "Companies can locate anywhere now. You don't have to be the factory down by the river. They're looking for the quality of life, and the previous administrations have all done a good job of improving the quality of life in Anchorage, whether it's trail connections, park lands, the Project 80s facilities, which clearly have to be upgraded for a new generation of users. Those are the sort of things that people like, living in a city with those amenities. I like going to the PAC to see West Side Story, or to the Shootout at the arena, or we skate down at the lagoon on Sundays."

Begich said, "Each mayor came in to improve the city that they lived in. We had our own ways of doing it. Each one of us looked at the city and said, how could we improve it, not only for this generation, but for the next generation?"

People make a city and a city makes a certain kind of person. In these two sons of Anchorage, who were chosen by Anchorage voters to lead, we can look for the qualities the city produces. Their fifty-plus years of life in Anchorage traverse half the story of the centennial.

Dan Sullivan was born in Fairbanks, the third of nine children of George and Margaret Sullivan. George, who was born in Valdez in 1922 and went to work at a young age, was a gifted teller of stories about frontier days. He lived and served in office in Fairbanks and Nenana before coming to Anchorage in 1959. In Nenana, he was the U.S. Marshal from 1946 to 1952, while his wife, Margaret, was the U.S. Commissioner, essentially the judge. In their funny stories about those days the accused would lose hope when they realized the judge was the arresting officer's wife.

George Sullivan served briefly, by appointment, as a Republican in the State House in 1964, in 1965 he was elected to the Anchorage City Council, and he was elected mayor in 1967. The city's boundaries then reached only as far south as Northern Lights Boulevard, and the job of mayor remained part-time and mostly ceremonial. A city manager handled daily business. Sullivan worked for a trucking company. But he made the office of mayor as big a position as he could, building popularity while battling a borough government many downtown residents regarded as expensive and out of control.

During debate over unifying the city and borough, Sullivan pushed for a structure with a full-time, professional mayor. That issue proved to be the toughest fight of charter commission deliberations, with the strong-mayor system prevailing. When that new, strong mayor for the entire municipality was up for election in 1975, Sullivan won the job handily.

A tough political operator, he managed the difficult job of merging the city and borough governments and planned the next phase of the city's growth. He retired after reaching the new charter's two-term limit in 1981, having served 14 years in total, longer than any other mayor. And likely longer than any future mayor, given the term limit.

Mark Begich, like Dan Sullivan, came from a large Catholic family with blue-collar roots. He was the fourth of six children of Nick and Pegge Begich, who had moved from Minnesota in 1956. Nick was endlessly energetic, an educator who rose rapidly through the teacher's union and school district administration. During hours off, he built

*The Begich family, from left: Tom, father Nick Sr., Nick Jr. (rear), and Mark (front), Nichelle, baby Stephanie, and mother Pegge. A fourth son, Paul, is not pictured. Nick Sr. served in Congress. Mark served as mayor of Anchorage and U.S. Senator. Photograph courtesy of the Begich family.*

apartment buildings in east Anchorage, using his teacher friends as construction labor and creating an investment legacy for his family.

Nick Begich was only 31 years old when he was elected as a Democrat to the State Senate in 1963. He was 36 when he ran for Congress for the first time and 38 when he won. His single term as a member of the U.S. House of Representatives happened to come at one of the most important moments in Alaska's history, when the Alaska Native Claims Settlement Act passed and legislation to allow construction of the trans-Alaska oil pipeline came to life. Begich was known for his energy and intelligence working on these complex issues, despite being a freshman, and built a strong reputation among his colleagues and popularity back home.

In 1972, while campaigning for re-election, Nick Begich disappeared on a small plane flight from Anchorage to Juneau, along with U.S. House Majority Leader Hale Boggs, aide Russell Brown and pilot Don Jonz. The largest aerial search in U.S. history failed to find the plane, and no trace or major clue has been found to this day. Although presumably dead, Begich won re-election to the House, only to be replaced by Republican Don Young in a special election the following spring.

Mark Begich was a school kid in a Washington suburb of Virginia when his father disappeared. He remembers chaos descending on the big family home in McLean, with people bringing food and trying to help, and a call from President Nixon. But he was protected from the media and didn't fully comprehend the magnitude of what had happened.

"It was very busy, and quickly things evolved into us getting ready to come back to Alaska in December, late December, when they declared him officially dead," he recalled. "Coming here is where it all started to register. Because here is more public. We had the memorial service. We had a reception-type event. We had everything coming together, the written material and everything. But it was different. I wasn't reading the news. I was 10."

Pegge and the children moved into a new home in Geneva Woods and he began attending Lake Otis Elementary.

Dan Sullivan grew up on Twelfth Avenue, a dirt road at the time, across from Inlet View School, where he and his siblings all attended. At age 8 he started selling newspapers with his brother Harvey, a year older, roaming through the bar rooms and hotel lobbies on Fourth Avenue, and taking a baseball mitt along to play a pickup game at the fields on the Park Strip. The town was small and everyone knew everyone else. The Sullivan boys were free as long as they made it home in time for dinner.

"These were really idyllic days," he said. "You just cannot imagine what a great place it was to grow up. … With nine kids and one earning parent, we lived what now would probably be considered a lower middle class existence. But you just don't realize it at the time, because you're just busy-busy-busy. I'm just glad I didn't have older sisters, because the hand-me-downs were at least the right gender. Thanks Mom and Dad!"

Sullivan said having a Dad who was mayor never felt like a big deal. "I was pretty darn proud of him, more than anything else, and willing to defend him at a moment's notice, as scrappy Irish kids are."

Begich's warm early memories include the smell of ink from his father's campaign literature. In the early campaigns, a downstairs apartment in one of his father's buildings was set up as a mailing house, the kitchen shelves stacked with leaflets and the many children's hands stuffing the envelopes. He remembers watching bonfires of appliance boxes when his dad was building apartments, and crossing a creek in the undeveloped land near Boniface Parkway to go to kindergarten in a log cabin.

But after his father's death, Begich grew up rapidly. He was among the first students who attended Steller Secondary School, a grade 7-12 open-concept alternative school that encouraged non-traditional, individualized learning. He was an average student, but he took advantage of the freedom the school offered to get involved in business ventures.

As a teenager he rented hotel ballrooms to put on teen disco dancing parties, and that developed into opening a teen nightclub on Ingra Street. By the time he graduated from high school, Begich was involved in various businesses, including running the family's apartments. As his siblings left for college, he stayed behind, too involved in business to care much about college, and too needed by the family to leave.

Dan Sullivan's father, as mayor, started Mark Begich in politics. He answered an ad to be on the city's Youth Advisory Commission and received the mayor's appointment. That inspired him to apply for a city job as youth programs coordinator.

When Mayor Tony Knowles was elected in 1981, he offered a weekly open door period. "You could go up there and complain about stuff, and so I kept sending young people up there," Begich said. One day the mayor's chief of staff called and asked him to come see the mayor, who asked him

*Lydia Perensovich and Bridget McCleskey on the Tony Knowles Coastal Trail near Point Woronzof in September, 2011. Photograph by Bob Hallinen, Alaska Dispatch News.*

to become his personal aid. "I didn't apply. I didn't even know why the heck I was going up there. I thought I was getting fired. Because I'd caused a lot of trouble."

At 20, Begich found himself spending his days with the mayor, handling his schedule, attending events, driving his car, and giving advice. Six years later, he ran for the Assembly, supported by his poker buddies, some teachers he had worked with, and his future wife, Deborah Bonito. The year, 1988, was at the depths of Anchorage's real estate depression.

"When I did door to door, every third house was occupied," he recalled. "It was like a ghost town in some places. Unbelievably huge despair. People had left town. Banks were closing. …The economy collapsed. So being in the apartment business was no fun. It required me to learn the trade very quickly. I ended up doing a lot of maintenance work, repairs myself, renting the units, everything, while I was running for office."

Begich won from a crowded field of candidates and served the limit of three Assembly terms, ten years in office, becoming a leader and deal-maker, and frequently a thorn in the side of mayors Tom Fink and Rick Mystrom. Throughout that period, he carried tools in his car, so he could quickly switch from a political meeting to deal with a tenant's plumbing problems.

Sullivan's west side Republican family mirrored Begich's east side Democratic family. He was slower to get into politics on his own, but he, too, worked in politics as the family business. As a high school junior, he helped his dad run for mayor the first time, and then he repeated the tasks every three years for the next 14.

"He was the first candidate who did the sign-waving on the corner, so curse him for that," Dan joked.

A stand-out basketball player at West High, Sullivan led the team as captain at a time when basketball was capable of gripping the city and cross-town rivalries were intense. In the 1969 state championship tournament, Sullivan's West High team beat a superior East High team coached by the legendary Chuck White in double overtime, a game the details of which the two men were able to discuss decades later. West then lost in overtime to a Fairbanks team. Sullivan was an exceptional tennis player, too.

George Sullivan with daughter Colleen and son Dan. George and his wife Margaret also had sons Timothy, Harvey, Kevin, George Jr., Michael, Casey, and daughter Shannon. George and Dan both served as mayor of Anchorage. Photograph courtesy of the Sullivan family.

Sullivan attended the University of Oregon and earned a bachelor's degree in political science. Back in Anchorage, he partnered with his father and his brother Harvey in 1986 to start the Sullivan Group, lobbying for Marathon Oil, the National Federation of Businesses and other clients, and doing business consulting.

But he also kept pursuing his interest in sports and recreation, running the box office at the Sullivan Arena and managing a branch of the Alaska Club fitness centers. During the 1990s, he spent three years as executive director of the Arctic Winter Games in Chugiak-Eagle River, and brought off the international event with a profit that allowed the organization to refund a $100,000 grant to the municipality. He later opened McGinley's Pub, with partners, an Irish bar and restaurant across the parking lot from City Hall.

When Sullivan got around to running for the Assembly in 1999, he was 47 years old. His father had been out of office long enough that the family name had lost much of its political potency. His opponent, former school board member Harriet Drummond, had higher name recognition in early polls. But Sullivan was supported by Mayor Mystrom, who broke a personal rule to publicly endorse him and recorded a radio ad on his behalf.

Politics tends to categorize people into teams, and Sullivan, like Mystrom, was a Republican and fell on the conservative side of the spectrum of supposedly non-partisan city elections. In his 1999 campaign he criticized Drummond's spending on the school board and talked about holding down the city budget. But he also campaigned on creating more programs for youth, cutting fees at recreation centers and building a new center in south Anchorage, and was involved in a recycling organization and wanted to pursue curbside service.

He won the race against Drummond and never had to worry about holding the west Anchorage seat, serving the maximum three terms on the Assembly. He was a conservative leader, and, when Begich became mayor in 2003, became a strong Assembly counter-weight on many issues.

The two mayors have substantive differences, especially in their approach to relations with city employee unions and on social issues, such as gay rights. Begich was more aggressive about building new roads and facilities and Sullivan focused more on establishing solid city finances.

Late October, 2005, at Potter Marsh. Photograph by Jim Lavrakas, Anchorage Dispatch News.

Both mayors felt their predecessors left them with a financial mess to resolve and both felt they succeeded, pointing to the city's excellent bond rating as evidence. Under Mayor Sullivan the credit rating hit the maximum level, higher than the U.S. government's. They both wanted the things many voters want: good roads and schools, safe streets, well-kept parks and low taxes.

Their personalities are not the same, of course. Sullivan is funny and warm in person, but low key in groups and was known on the Assembly for rarely initiating legislative deals. Begich lights up in front of groups and loves working out compromises with colleagues, but rarely seems to slow down. There is much they have in common, too—an Anchorage factor. Both men are clearly comfortable with different kinds of people. Neither yells nor pushes; a calm, casual way of speaking is always preferred, even in conflict. Each is easier to imagine shoveling his driveway than leading a political rally.

Anchorage people get along. They prioritize being nice. The city's politics can be quite heated, but voters don't like leaders who get mad or take things too seriously. The consensus is too strong for that. Anchorage local government is supposed to make the town better, a bit at a time, to build on the good luck that has blessed the city so far, and to avoid spending too much money.

The city has matured. As Sullivan noted, it looks better these days with every building season, as the expedient construction of the past is replaced with more thoughtfully designed structures, as landscaping grows, and as community standards evolve. Economically, a city that grew in bursts and crumpled in slumps now has enough different industries that no single event has significantly diverted its gradual upward path in decades. The city stands on many legs besides state oil revenue: military spending, Native corporation and oil company headquarters, hub medical facilities, tourism, a port serving most of the state, and an airport that is fourth worldwide in cargo tonnage.

Sullivan said the city's success all fits together.

"I think it was natural that this becomes the headquarters city, because we've got quality of life here that is pretty darn good. Then you throw in the awestruck beauty of the place, and all those things kind of blend in to making a pretty strong city that I think can weather any downturns, not to say there's never going to be some painful moments.

"But the thing is, going forward, I don't think it's just going to be the result now of being a mature city, I think it's going to be companies looking for good places for their businesses to be, for their employees, and for their economic opportunities. And we are starting to hear more and more about people looking at Anchorage as their headquarters. I think it was a maturing thing at first, but now I think it is going to be more strategic.

"I never look at Alaska as a state. We're a country. Look at who we trade with. We trade with China, Japan, Korea, Taiwan. We're a Pacific Rim nation, by all standards."

When Sullivan and Begich talk about the future of the city, they seem to see a similar place.

Begich said, "Anchorage continues to grow as an international city in a lot of ways, not only from its make-up of who it is, but also what we do, from air cargo and other work we do. We will continue to be a very international city from that perspective. Also, I think Anchorage will continue to be a place that people discover and want to go to live.

"And I also think Anchorage will continue to be one of these cities that no matter who you are, where you come from, how much you make, what your social status is, you can make anything happen. I really believe that, because of the way the city operates. I think that's a powerful part of Anchorage and will continue to be Anchorage."

# Acknowledgments

Without the help of extraordinary people, this book would not exist. I especially thank David Holthouse, my primary contact at the Alaska Humanities Forum and first-line editor. His talent and strength were exceptional. Courtney Farnham's many hours of cheerful effort researching photographs saved the project when the pressure of the oncoming centennial deadline loomed. Earlier in the project Gretchen Sagan and Pennelope Goforth contributed their significant talents.

During writing and after completion of the manuscript I received support from peer reviewers (although I am far from being a peer with these illustrious Alaskans). Professor Emeritus Stephen Haycox did an early read very quickly, which was exceptionally helpful. Jim Barnett did a close read through the entire manuscript with scores of helpful comments. Jack Roderick not only read and advised, but also provided additional material and helped work through difficult passages on oil. Vic Fischer read and marked up many chapters and provided important comments. Professor Terrence Cole provided detailed comments that prevented errors and improved the text. John Cloe read the military chapters, corrected errors, and provided much unpublished information.

Of course, responsibility for the text and any remaining errors is my own.

A number of organizations made the book possible. The project started and ended with an enjoyable collaboration with Flip Todd of Todd Communications. The Alaska Humanities Forum, ably led by Nina Kemppel, provided financial and practical support. Through the forum, the Municipality of Anchorage funded the centennial activities, of which this book is a part. The Anchorage Museum helped with photographs from its archives. *The Alaska Dispatch News* allowed the unique use of its photo files. The support of photo editor Anne Raup was truly extraordinary and is deeply appreciated, as well as that of Tony Hopfinger, Pat Dougherty and David Hulen. Mary Barry shared her personal collection of photographs by Sydney Laurence and Nellie Brown. I also received great help from Douglas Beckstead, historian of the 673rd Air Base Wing History Office, Joint Base Elemendorf-Richardson.

The Anchorage Public Library holds the heart of the city's history in its indispensable Alaska Collection. The staff there was repeatedly helpful. Circulation supervisor Debra Milam assisted me with keeping current with the many volumes I needed. Bruce Merrell, although retired from the library, remains my go-to bibliographer whenever I start a project, and he was essential for this as for previous of my books, guiding me to the right sources and even lending me some of his invaluable files.

The individuals who helped are too many to mention. John McKay provided key support at a critical time. Many sources are listed in the book and the notes. They gave their time and, in many cases, opened their lives, to help create a book that would record essential Anchorage stories for the centennial. I made several new friends and called on some old friends. I am deeply grateful to Jim Fall, Mary Barry, Brooke Marston, Jim LaBelle, Jane Angvik, Connie Yoshimura, and Indra Arriaga for their time and openness.

# Chapter Notes

As a popular book, *From the Shores of Ship Creek, Stories of Anchorage's First 100 Years,* does not have footnotes, but the author verified facts from original documents, published sources, interviews by the author and others, newspaper articles, government reports and other sources. In a few cases, the author's personal experience as a lifelong Anchorage resident was a primary source. For readers and scholars who want to learn more, or investigate sources, this section provides chapter-by-chapter notes.

The author conducted more than 30 interviews. Those sources are attributed in the text and are not repeated here. In addition, he used interviews he previously recorded with several people on earlier projects, including Walter Hickel, Vic Fischer, Dave Rose, Frank Reed and others. Most of that material is in the author's possession, although his 1990s interviews with Hickel are in the University of Alaska Anchorage Archives. The "Anchorage Pioneers Oral History Project," by Stephen Haycox, assisted by Maureen Cowles, also was an invaluable source of quotations and facts. From 1992 to 1995, Haycox interviewed 30 early Anchorage residents. His report and transcripts are held in the University of Alaska Anchorage Archives.

## Chapter 1 notes

The best source on the traditional Dena'ina culture in general and Shem Pete in particular is the classic *Shem Pete's Alaska: The Territory of the Upper Cook Inlet Dena'ina, 2nd edition,* by James Kari and James A. Fall, principal contributor Shem Pete (Fairbanks: University of Alaska Press, 2003). Information also came from a paper, "An Overview of Dena'ina Athabascan Uses of Sites on and near Elmendorf Air Force Base, Alaska," by James A. Fall, Nancy Yaw Davis, and the Dena'ina Team, prepared for U.S Army Corps of Engineers, June 2003. Fall also provided extensive personal communication.

For the story of meeting of the Dena'ina and Captain Cook, and its impact, a much more complete account is found in the author's book, *The Fate of Nature: Rediscovering Our Ability to Rescue the Earth* (New York: St. Martin's Press, 2010). The story of Captain James Cook's 1778 visit to the Anchorage area is told authoritatively in J.C. Beaglehole, *The Life of Captain James Cook* (Stanford: Stanford University Press, 1974). More interesting detail comes from *The Journals of Captain James Cook on His Voyages of Discovery: The Voyage of the* Resolution *and* Discovery, J.C. Beaglehole, ed. (Woodbridge, England: Boydell Press, 1999).

## Chapter 2 notes

The author conducted extensive original research on Langille and the Ballinger-Pinchot Affair for his book *The Fate of Nature,* cited in notes for Chapter 1. Detailed notes in that book will guide the reader to original documents on Langille, Pinchot, the controversy and the region, found in the University of Oregon Library, the Library of Congress and the National Archives, including letters, diaries, articles and reports. Various National Forest Service reports, letters and memoranda quoted in the chapters 2 and 3 were found in the National Archives in Record Group 95 in Anchorage; those files are currently being moved to Seattle. An excellent overview is *A History of the United States Forest Service in Alaska,* by Lawrence Rakestraw (1981; Juneau: USDA Forest Service, 2002).

Many books cover the Ballinger-Pinchot Affair, each with its own perspective. The best overall source on Pinchot is *Gifford Pinchot and the Making of Modern Environmentalism,* by Char Miller (Washington, D.C.: Island Press/Shearwater Books, 2001). Pinchot's autobiography is also informative and a good read, *Breaking New Ground* (1947; Washington, D.C.: Island Press, 1998). A clear review of the facts, but entirely taking Ballinger's point of view, is *Progressive Politics and Conservation: The Ballinger-Pinchot Affair,* by James Penick Jr. (Chicago: University of Chicago Press, 1968).

The very best source on the founding and early years of the Alaska Railroad and the federal years of early Anchorage is *Railroad in the Clouds: The Alaska Railroad in the Age of Steam, 1914-1945,* by William H. Wilson (Boulder, Colo.: Pruett Publishing Co., 1977). The quotation from Taft's message to Congress, from Wickersham's speech, and some other events leading up the Alaska Railroad Act, are covered in *Frontier Politics: Alaska's James Wickersham,* by Evangeline Atwood (Portland: Binford and Mort, 1979).

## Chapter 3 notes

Many of the sources in Chapter 2 were essential in Chapter 3 as well, especially Wilson's *Railroad in the Clouds,* which is the best source on Andrew Christensen. Filmmaker Todd Hardesty turned up Christensen's May 20, 1935, letter to *Time.* But the most important sources were the annual reports of the Alaska Engineering Commission and the related letters and memoranda, found in the National Archives, in the records of the Alaska Railroad. The future site of these files is undetermined at this writing.

Material on the Alaska Engineering Commission's conflict with the Forest Service is mostly from Forest Service records, cited in Chapter 2 notes. Grave's diary is found in the Henry Solon Graves Papers at the Yale University Library.

*Jack and Nellie Brown: pioneer settlers of Anchorage Alaska,* by Mary J. Barry (self-published, c2000), was an invaluable source on their lives. Jack Brown's handwritten diary, with those of other forest guards of the time, were found in Record Group 95 in the National Archives in Anchorage, but are also scheduled to be moved.

The quote from McCutcheon is from the Haycox oral history mentioned above. Zula Wester's obituary was published by the *Anchorage Times* January 13, 1973.

### Chapter 4 notes

Mary Barry's book on Jack and Nellie Brown, cited in Chapter 3 notes, provided invaluable support to Chapter 4, as did personal communications with Barry. Other key sources included Wilson's *Railroad in the Clouds* and Haycox's Anchorage Pioneer Oral History Project, both cited above. The material on race, the quotation from Bob Atwood, and the story of private road construction toward Palmer all come from Haycox.

Cotton's report to Lane is in the Alaska Railroad records in the National Archives, mentioned in Chapter 3 notes. Christensen's quotations and the railroad's financial details come from the same files.

Elizabeth Tower's *Anchorage: From Its Humble Origins as a Railroad Construction Camp* (Fairbanks and Seattle: Epicenter Press, 1999) contains a handy profile of Sydney Laurence and a variety of other early figures.

### Chapter 5 notes

Frank Reed material comes from the Haycox oral history and from interviews with the author, including a December 7, 2011, Alaska Public Media interview specifically on his World War II experiences, found at http://www.alaskapublic.org/2011/12/02/anchorage-in-world-war-ii/ (accessed June 13, 2014). Information on Bill and Lilian Stolt and Steve McCutcheon also comes from Haycox's project.

The main source for construction of bases and for the war was *Top Cover for America: The Air Force in Alaska 1920-1983,* by John Cloe with Michael F. Monaghan (Anchorage Chapter – Air Force Association, 1984). Cloe also provided extensive written personal communications. Many other books and articles on this period are available and provided details,

including Terrence Cole's "Boom Town: Anchorage and the Second World War," in *Journal of the West,* July, 1986. For the economic impact of the military in Alaska, and the best overall economic history of the state, see Cole's report "Blinded by Riches: The Permanent Funding Problem and the Prudhoe Bay Effect," for the University of Alaska Institute of Social and Economic Research, January 2004.

The detail about Ernest Gruening interceding to allow Native women in USO facilities comes from *Men of the Tundra: Alaska Eskimos at War,* by Muktuk Marston (New York, October House, 1969). Gruening covers this period and civil rights in detail in his own *Many Battles: The Autobiography of Ernest Gruening* (New York: Liveright, 1973).

Information on the development of electric power and the Reeds' power plant comes from "The Early Electrification of Anchorage," by Kristy Hollinger, a report for the Center for Environmental Management of Military Lands at Colorado State University, July 2002.

### Chapter 6 notes

A series typescripts provided by Chris Tower Zafren provided the core of information about Helen Whaley, John Tower and other medical pioneers in Anchorage; these documents were the text of presentations made by John Tower to the Cook Inlet Historical Society, May 1999, and an unpublished memoir, which is undated. The published materials included three essays in a series by Gwynneth Gminder Wilson, "History of Medicine in Alaska," in *Alaska Medicine,* which covered John Tower (Vol. 30, no. 1, Jan-Feb 1988); Robert Whaley (Vol. 28, no. 4, Oct-Dec 1986); and women in medicine in Anchorage (Vol. 33, no. 4, Oct-Dec 1991). The author also was fortunate to interview Robert Whaley shortly before his death.

*Alaska Native Medical Center: A History,* by Robert Fortuine (Anchorage: Alaska Native Medical Center, 1986) was invaluable on the center itself and the state of health care in Alaska in the 1950s generally.

Military history of the Cold War comes primarily from Cloe, sources cited in Chapter 5 notes. The fear induced by the conflict was informed by the author's memories and by Peter Dunlap-Shohl's video "How Alaska Won the Cold War," found at LitSite Alaska (litsite.org, accessed June 13, 2014).

Information on Charles Brewster comes from a report held in the Anchorage Public Library, "Interviews with Alaskans," by James Gary Stoops and Noel Grunwaldt, for the Anchorage School District, 1998. Most of the information on Walter Hickel is from author interviews, cited above. Readers can learn more about Hickel's extraordinary life from two autobiographies: *Who Owns America?* (Englewood Cliffs, New Jersey: Prentice-Hall, 1971), and *Crisis in the Commons: The Alaska Solution* (Oakland: Institute for Contemporary Studies, 2002).

Aviation history is from "Frontier Flight," an edition of *Alaska Geographic* (Vol. 25, no. 4). Material on the Anchorage Independent School District is from "Aspects of Growth and Change in the Anchorage Independent School District Between 1952 and 1964," a book-length report by Caroline P. Wohlforth (mother of this book's author) for the Alaska State Historical Commission, undated. It is found the Anchorage Public Library.

## Chapter 7 notes

Robert Atwood's memories and quotations are drawn from three sources: *Bob Atwood's Alaska: The Memoirs of a Legendary Newspaper Man* (Anchorage: self-published, 2003); the Haycox oral history cited above; and the "Interviewing Alaskans" document cited in chapter 6 notes.

Atwood's friend, Vic Fischer, also provided information in interviews and in *To Russia With Love: An Alaskan's Journey,* by Vic Fischer with Charles Wohlforth (Fairbanks: University of Alaska Press, 2012). Gruening's autobiography, cited in chapter 5 notes, was used extensively here. The author interviewed Katie Hurley March 17, 2010, for the Fischer project.

Ted Stevens' biography remains to be written, but he participated in a series of biographic articles by David Whitney in the *Anchorage Daily News,* published in August 1994. An installment titled "Seeking Statehood," August 10, 1994, covers Stevens' efforts at Interior.

## Chapter 8 notes

Jack Roderick provided invaluable interviews and extensive other information on Locke Jacobs and 1950s oil leasing. The story is well told in his now-classic *Crude Dreams: A Personal History of Oil & Politics in Alaska* (Fairbanks and Seattle: Epicenter Press, 1997). Of particular help, he provided a transcript of an interview about Jacobs with John and MayJean McManamin, conducted December 2, 2000, by Andrew McCoy.

A series of articles, "Inside Deal," in the *Anchorage Daily News* February 4 to February 11, 1990, by David Postman, is the most complete and deeply researched version of the events surrounding the leasing of the Swanson River Oil Field. Some of Postman's conclusions are debatable, but the factual basis of the series is solid. The quotation from Vic Fischer is from an interview for *To Russia with Love* (see Chapter 7 notes), where his most complete version of the story is told.

## Chapter 9 notes

Brooke Marston proved to be a remarkable interview subject. The heart of the chapter comes from an afternoon spent with him March 7, 2014. Muktuk Marston's *Men of the Tundra,* cited under Chapter 5 notes, was also a source. Julia Person's memories of Wilda Marston's role are found in *Where Were You? Alaska 64 Earthquake,* Joy Griffen, ed. (Homer: Homer Public Library, 1996).

Readers may notice that McCollie Avenue is spelled differently than J.H. McCallie's name, although it was named for him. The spelling of McCallie comes from John Bagoy's biographic reference *Legends and Legacies: Anchorage 1910-1935* (Anchorage: Publication Consultants, c2001). Brooke Marston was unsure why the spelling of the street is different, as it was intended to honor McCallie.

The 1959 USGS report is *Surficial Geology of Anchorage and Vicinity Alaska: Geological Survey Bulletin 1093,* by Robert D. Miller and Ernest Dobrovolny (Washington, D.C.: Government Printing Office, 1959).

A conceptual overview of the quake and facts about the slides came from a March 20, 2014, lecture by Kristine Crossen of the University of Alaska Anchorage, Department of Geology, at the Anchorage Museum. The emergency response and initial reconstruction is covered in many sources, including Fischer's *To Russia With Love,* cited above, and *Saving for the Future: My Life and the Alaska Permanent Fund,* by Dave Rose, as told to Charles Wohlforth (Fairbanks and Seattle: Epicenter Press, 2008).

The quake was extraordinarily well studied, as was the story of how the community ignored the advice of experts afterward. Two essays on those subjects are found in *The Great Alaska Earthquake of 1964: Human Ecology* (Washington, D.C.: National Academy of Sciences, 1970), which is one of eight volumes the Academy published on the quake. These informative essays are: "The Work of the Science and Engineering Task Force," by Edwin B. Eckel and William E. Schaem, and, most important, "Urban Planning in the Reconstruction," by Lidia Selkregg, Edwin B. Crittenden, and Norman Williams, Jr. The quotation from Sewell "Stumpy" Faulkner is from his self-published *Stumpy's Diary 1964: A Year in the Life of an Anchorage Family: And what a year!,* edited and produced by Lewis Turner (Anchorage, 1987).

Updating the reconstruction issue for another generation, an article published for the 25th anniversary of the quake provided the political story: "64 quake danger still lurks beneath the surface," by Don Hunter, in the *Anchorage Daily News,* March 26, 1989, which contains the quotations from Cliff Groh and Carl Brady. Dr. Sheila Selkregg's dissertation, *The decision and rationale which led to construction on high-risk land after the 1964 Alaska earthquake: analysis of risk-based cultural dissociation,* was submitted to Portland State University in 1994, and a copy is housed at the Anchorage Public Library.

## Chapter 10 notes

Jim LaBelle provided much of the content of the chapter in a series of interviews with the author. Details on passage of the Alaska Native Claims Settlement Act, especially the role of Ted Stevens and Anchorage leaders, came from *Take My Land, Take My Life,* by Don Mitchell (Fairbanks: University of Alaska Press, 2001).

Besides LaBelle's comments, material on Chugach Alaska land selections and business activities came from various articles by Hal Bernton in the *Anchorage Daily News* in the late 1980s and early '90s. Information on Cook Inlet Region Inc.'s real estate dealings comes primarily from the CIRI-sponsored 2006 report, "Cook Inlet Land Exchange 30-year Anniversary," which is found at http://www.ciri.com/wpcontent/uploads/2013/12/Oct06_LandExchange.pdf (accessed June 15, 2014).

Details and quotations on the urban-rural divide come largely from newspaper coverage, particularly "Urban-rural divide widens in Juneau," by Tom Kizzia, in *Anchorage Daily News,* May 3, 1998, where the quotations from Roy Huhndorf and Ramona Barnes are found.

## Chapter 11 notes

Many interviews contributed to the account of borough and city conflict and unification. Besides her informative interview, Jane Angvik provided extensive notes, articles and minutes from the Charter Commission. In addition, the author did extensive newspaper and documentary research for a more detailed telling of the story in *Saving for the Future,* the Dave Rose autobiography cited in Chapter 9 notes. That's the most detailed history of the unification fight available. A remarkable book by Wellesley sociologist Lee J. Cuba captures the times and residents' attitudes, using surveys and careful observation: *Identity and Community on the Alaskan Frontier* (Philadelphia: Temple University Press, 1987).

The story of local government in the Alaska Constitution is covered in Fischer's *To Russia with Love,* cited above. The USGS report on Spenard groundwater is cited in Chapter 9 notes. Numerous details on the development of boroughs, including Anchorage's, are found in *The Metropolitan Experiment in Alaska: A study of borough government,* by Ronald C. Cease (New York: Praeger, 1968). Egan's quote is from that volume. Dick Fischer's essay in Cease's book, although partisan, is informative.

The quotations from a speech and editorial from the time of the opening of the John M. Asplund Wastewater Treatment Plant are from a two-page history published by the Anchorage Water and Wastewater Utility, which is online at https://www.awwu.biz/website/Wastewater/JohnMAsplund_TreatmentPlantHistory_Final.pdf (accessed June 15, 2014).

## Chapter 12 notes

Economic analysis and statistics on the 1980s boom and bust in Anchorage come primarily from publications by O. Scott Goldsmith, et al, in the series "Alaska Review of Social and Economic Conditions," published by the University of Alaska Anchorage Institute of Social and Economic Research, including from the editions of December, 1987 (Vol. XXIV, No. 2); February 1988 (Vol. XXV, No. 1); May 1988 (Vol. XXV, No. 2); June 1989 (Vol. XXVI, No. 2); and June 1990 (Vol. XXVII, No. 1).

Details of projects advanced during Mayor Tony Knowles' time in office come from a municipal report he lent to the author, "Municipality of Anchorage 1982-1987: The Growth Years."

## Chapter 13 notes

Putting together the story of why Anchorage has become more diverse involved discussion, analysis and communications with several economists and demographers, including Eddie Hunsinger and Neal Fried of the Alaska Department of Labor and Chad Farrell of the University of Alaska Anchorage. Hunsinger helped with analytical work to look at various theories, and he provided a number of useful articles from the department's "Alaska Economic Trends" newsletter.

The 1987-88 Martin Luther King Jr. naming controversy is covered in a series of articles in the *Anchorage Daily News.* Quotations from Williams and Connerty are from "Defending a Name," by Debbie McKinney, in *Anchorage Daily News,* September 9, 1986. The article on the pulpit swap that inspired Mystrom to found Bridge Builders was "A Joyful Noise," by Tom Bell, in *Anchorage Daily News,* March 31, 1996. Malcolm and Cindy Roberts gave a helpful interview; Mayor Rick Mystrom's quotation about Malcolm is from "The Assistant Mayor," by Sheila Toomey, in *Anchorage Daily News,* November 2, 1997.

Rick Mystrom's autobiography focuses on his diabetes, but also contains concise accounts of several events covered here: *My Wonderful Life with Diabetes: An Inspiring and Empowering Story of Living Healthy, Living Active, and Living Well with Diabetes* (Anchorage: Tadfield Publishing, 2013).

## Chapter 14 notes

The chapter is based on interviews with Mayor Dan Sullivan and Senator Mark Begich, as well as newspaper coverage and the author's memories from their periods of service.